FIRST WORDS

Linda Mrowicki

Photography by:

Daniel C. Jackson
Scott Jackson

Illustrations and cover design by:

Sally Richardson

LINMORE PUBLISHING

Box 1545   Palatine, IL 60078   (815) 223-7499

Linmore Publishing
P.O. Box 1545
Palatine, IL 60078
(815) 223-7499

© Linmore Publishing, Inc. 1990
First printing, 1990
Printed in the United States of America

FIRST WORDS
Student's Book   ISBN 0-916591-21-2
Teacher's Resource Book   ISBN 0-916591-22-0

ACKNOWLEDGMENTS

This book was created with the help of many people who offered creative suggestions, support, and encouragement. Especially appreciated are:

Peggy Dean whose interest is native and second language literacy provided a good sounding-board for addressing literacy issues.

Cheryl Harling who encouraged me and helped me at the creation stage

Janet Isserlis whose experience with low-level students and great sense of humor improved the lessons and my sense of humor as well.

K. Lynn Savage who has always been willing to share her expert views on language acquisition.

I am especially appreciative of the assistance provided by businesses in Palatine and Barrington. Their willingness to allow us to take photos indicated their great interest in and support of education.

The participation in the photography of the **staff and students of the World Relief - Du Page ESL Program** was very important. Their photos make the lessons come alive! Special thanks is extended to **Marilyn Sweeney** who patiently and enthusiastically organized the photography. The photographs could not have been completed without their help!

The following people kindly allowed themselves to be photographed:

Diane G. Brown
Andrew, Carolyn, and **Tabatha Cetwinski**
Julie and **Nancy Cirmo**
Aline Dolatowski, Palatine Post Office
Sidney Johnson, Bookseller
Fritz Klein, Kookers
Naly Khotavong
Jo Ann Lara, 1st Nationwide Bank of Palatine
Bhia Lao
The **Long** and **Kue** families
Julia and **Pedro Marroquin,** Marroquin Restaurant;
  Arturo Marroquin and **Evette Valdez, Connie Francis**
  and **Gilbert Martinez**

Chandra, Deatra, and **Dooney Marshall**
Genevieve, Jim, and **Joseph Mrowicki**
Tran Nhan
Thea Noegel, Edelweiss Delicatessen
Harriet S. Schneider
Jose and **Teresa Serrato**
Ed Smith, Parcel Service Center
Marilyn Sweeney
Lorrie Vavak, Phase II Resale
Song Xiong
Yia Yang

CONTENTS

1: NAMES

Listen to your teacher.

Practice with your teacher.

Read. Fill in. Copy.

NAME   N A M E   _____

name   n a m e   _____

Find FIRST.
Find MIDDLE.
Find LAST.

MAIN HIGH SCHOOL
Student Identification Card

1989-1990

Name ___Savin___ --- ___Khem___
First   Middle   Last

Read. Fill in. Copy.

FIRST F I R S T _____

first F i r S T _____

MIDDLE M I D D L E _____

middle m i d d l e _____

LAST L A S T _____

last L a s t _____

LETTER AND SOUND PRACTICE.

Write the words with ST.

F I R st
L A st

Write the words with M.

m I D D L E
n a m e

READING PRACTICE.
Read. Write.

NAME	Bilal
FIRST NAME	Bilal
LAST NAME	SULEMAN
Name	Bilal
Last Name	Suleman
First Name	Bilal
Middle Name	Omer
LAST NAME	SULEMAN
Last name	SULEMAN
MIDDLE NAME	Omer
Middle Name	omer
First Name	Bilal
Middle Name	omer
Last Name	Suleman
FIRST NAME	Bilal
Last Name	vuleman
First Name	Bilal

Read. Write. Remember.

NAME Bilal SULEMAN

3

SPEAKING PRACTICE.

Practice with a student.

| Hello. | Hi. |
| What's your name? | Roberto Sanchez. |

What's your first name?	Roberto.
What's your middle name?	Luis.
What's your last name?	Sanchez.

Student A

What's your name?

What's your first name?

What's your middle name?

What's your last name?

Student B

Bilal Suleman

Bilal.

Omer

Suleman

Write your answers. Remember them.

2: ALPHABET

Fill in. Say and practice.

A a	B b	C c	D d	E e
F f	G g	H h	I i	J j
K k	L l	M m	N n	O o
P p	Q q	R r	S s	T t
U u	V v	W w	X x	Y y
Z z				

SPEAKING PRACTICE.

Practice with a student.

What's your name?   Roberto Sanchez.

Can you spell your last name, please?   S A N C H E Z.

Thank you.   You're welcome.

Student A

What's your name?

Can you spell your last name, please?

Can you spell your first name, please?

Student B

Roberta sanchez

SANCHEZ.

You're welcome

6

3: SCHOOL

Circle SCHOOL.

Read. Fill in. Copy.

SCHOOL

S C H _O_ _O_ L

_____

School

S c h _o_ _o_ l

_____

Teacher

T e a c h e r

_____

Student

S t u d e n t

_____

Read. Write. Remember.

School's Name _____

Teacher's Name _ms hortie_

7

READING PRACTICE.

Say the words.

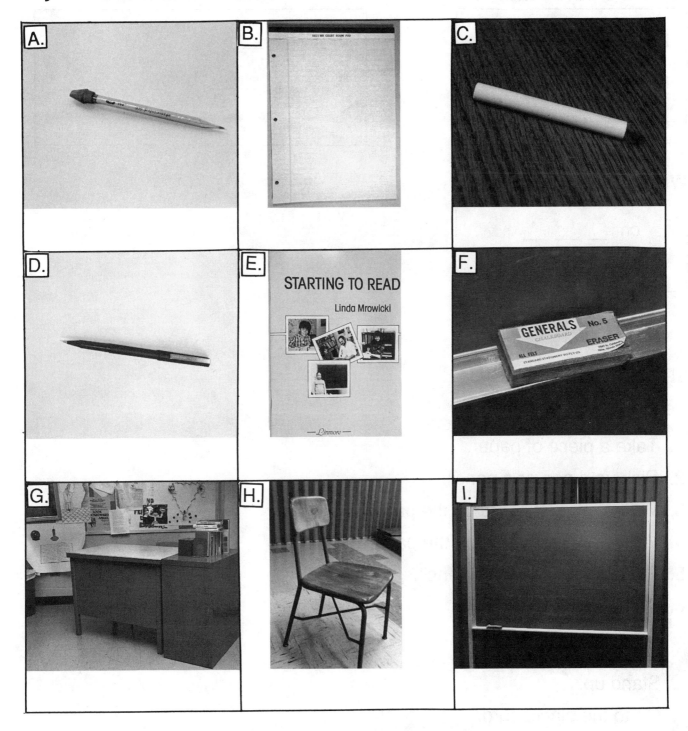

Read.

book	paper	pen	desk	eraser
chair	blackboard	chalk	pencil	

Write the words under the pictures.

8

SOUND AND LETTER PRACTICE.

Write the words with P.

p _ p _ _

p _ _

p _ _ _ _ _

Write the words with B.

b _ _ _

b _ _ _ _ b _ _ _ _

Write the words with CH.

ch _ _ _

ch _ _ _

SPEAKING PRACTICE.

Read and do.

1. Take a piece of paper.
2. Pick up a pen or a pencil.
3. Write your first name on the paper.
4. Write your last name on the paper.
5. Put down your pen or pencil.
6. Stand up.

1. Stand up.
2. Go to the blackboard.
3. Pick up a piece of chalk.
4. Write your first name.
5. Put down the chalk.
6. Go to your desk.
7. Sit down.

4: FAMILY

Listen to the teacher.

Practice with the teacher.

Read. Fill in. Copy.

FAMILY   __ A __ I L __   _____

family   __ a __ i l __   _____

Draw a line to the FATHER.   **Draw a line to the MOTHER.**

Draw a line to the DAUGHTER.   **Draw a line to the SON.**

Read. Fill in. Copy.

FATHER   __ __ T H E R   _____

father   __ __ t h e r   _____

MOTHER   __ __ T H E R   _____

mother   __ __ t h e r   _____

SON   __ O __   _____

son   __ o __   _____

DAUGHTER   __ A U G H __ __ __   _____

daughter   __ a u g h __ __ __   _____

11

Draw a line to the HUSBAND.   **Draw a line to the WIFE.**

HUSBAND   __ __ S B A __ __   _____

husband   __ __ s b a __ __   _____

WIFE   __ I F __   _____

wife   __ i f __   _____

Draw a line to the BROTHER.   **Draw a line to the SISTER.**

SISTER   __ I __ T E R   _____

sister   __ i __ t e r   _____

BROTHER   __ __ O T H __ __   _____

brother   __ __ o t h __ __   _____

12

LETTER AND SOUND PRACTICE.

Write the words with S.

s __ __

s __ __ __ __ __

Write the words with ER.

__ __ __ __ er

__ __ __ __ __ er

__ __ __ __ er

__ __ __ __ er

READING PRACTICE.
Read.

mother   father   husband   wife

sister   daughter   brother   son

Write the words under the pictures.

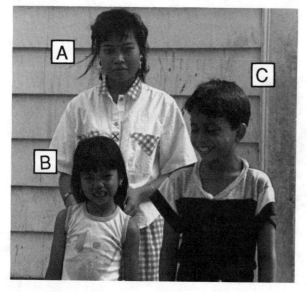

A and B:_____

A and C:_____

B and C:_____

A and B:_____

A and C:_____

B and C:_____

Write the correct words.

A and D:_____ C and D:_____

B and C:_____ A and C: _____

A and B:_____ B and D:_____

Read. Write. Remember.

Write the first names of your family.	Write the relationship.

SPEAKING PRACTICE.

Practice with a student.

What's your husband's name?	Shoua Vang.
What are your children's names?	Moua and Chong.

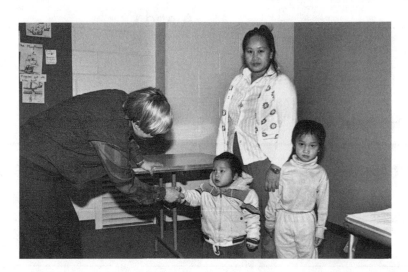

What's your father's name?	Shoua Vang.
What's your mother's name?	Bao Kue.

Student A   **Student B**

What's your _____'s name?   _____

What's your _____'s name?   _____

What are your _____'s names?   _____

Write your answers. Remember them.

END OF UNIT.

Fill out the form.

NAME

_____

First   Last

SCHOOL'S NAME _____

TEACHER'S NAME _____

NAMES OF PEOPLE IN YOUR FAMILY

_____

_____

_____

_____

_____

_____

_____

_____

_____

5: NUMBERS 0 - 10

Count. Fill in. Say and practice.

	0 _____
●	1 _____
● ●	2 _____
● ● ●	3 _____
● ● ● ●	4 _____
● ● ● ● ●	5 _____
● ● ● ● ● ●	6 _____
● ● ● ● ● ● ●	7 _____
● ● ● ● ● ● ● ●	8 _____
● ● ● ● ● ● ● ● ●	9 _____
● ● ● ● ● ● ● ● ● ●	10 _____

Count. Write the number.

A. ▲ ▲ ▲ ▲ ___	**B.** ✳ ✳ ___	**C.** ☐ ☐ ☐ ___
D. ✖ ✖ ✖ ✖ ✖ ✖ ✖ ✖ ✖ ✖ ___	**E.** ▮ ▮ ▮ ▮ ▮ ▮ ▮ ___	**F.** ● ● ● ● ● ___
G. ★ ___	**H.** ___	**I.** ✔ ✔ ✔ ✔ ✔ ✔ ✔ ✔ ✔ ___
J. ◆ ◆ ◆ ◆ ◆ ◆ ___	**K.** — — — — — — ___	**L.** ✳ ✳ ✳ ✳ ✳ ✳ ✳ ✳ ✳ ✳ ___

6: PERSONAL NUMBERS

Listen to the teacher.

Practice with the teacher.

Read. Fill in. Copy.

NUMBER   __ U __ B E R   _____

number   __ u __ b e r   _____

READING PRACTICE.
Circle SOCIAL SECURITY.

READ. FILL IN. COPY.

SOCIAL SECURITY

__ O C I A __

S __ __ U R I T __

__ U M B __ __

Read. Write.

1. SOCIAL SECURITY NUMBER _____

2. social security number _____

3. social security number _____

4. SOCIAL SECURITY NUMBER _____

5. Social Security # _____

6. Soc. Sec. No. __ __ __ __ __ __ __ __ __

7. soc. sec. no. ☐☐☐ — ☐☐ — ☐☐☐☐

8. SS # __ __ __ - __ __ - __ __ __ __

Read. Write. Remember.

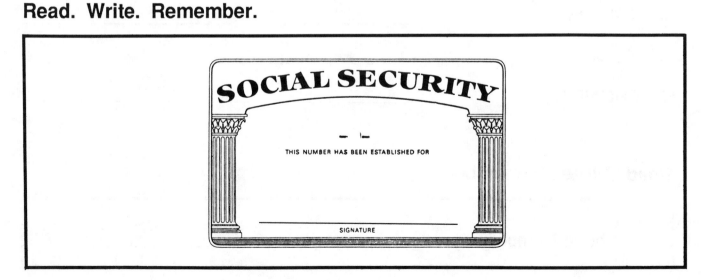

READING PRACTICE.

Circle PHONE.

READ. FILL IN.

PHONE

_ _ O _ E

TELEPHONE

_ E L E _ _ _ _ _

Read. Write.

1. TELEPHONE NUMBER (_____) _____

2. Telephone Number: _____

3. PHONE NUMBER: _____

4. Phone Number _____ _____ _____

5. Phone No. _____

6. TELEPHONE No. _____

7. phone # _____

8. TEL. No. _____

9. Tel. #: (_ _ _) _ _ _ - _ _ _ _

10. PHONE NO: _____

Read. Write. Remember.

Phone Number: _____

SPEAKING PRACTICE.

Practice with a student.

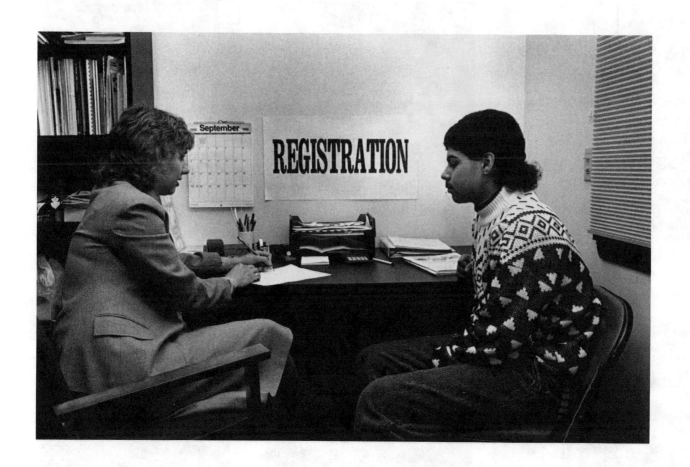

| What's your phone number? | 555-6857. |
| What's your social security number? | 453 - 57 - 4625. |

Student A

What's your phone number?

What's your social security number?

What's the school phone number?

Student B

_____

_____

_____

Write your answers. Remember them.

SPEAKING PRACTICE.

Listen to your teacher.

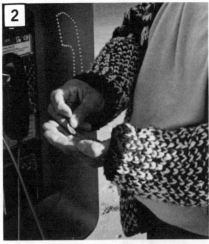

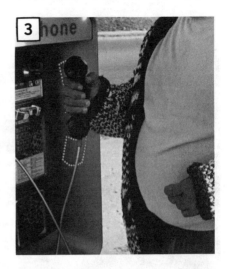

Say the instructions.

READING PRACTICE.

Read and do.

1. Go to the telephone.

2. Take out a quarter.

3. Pick up the telephone.

4. Put in the quarter.

5. Push the buttons for the phone number.

6. Listen.

7. Say hello and talk.

8. Say good-bye.

9. Put down the telephone.

Read and write.

1. Go to the t __ __ __ __ __ __ __ __.

2. T __ __ __ out a quarter.

3. P __ __ __ up the telephone.

4. P __ __ in the quarter.

5. P __ __ __ the buttons for the phone number.

6. Listen.

7. Say hello and t __ __ __.

8. Say good-bye.

9. Put down the t __ __ __ __ __ __ __ __.

Copy the sentences on a piece of paper.

7: NUMBERS 1 - 100

Fill in. Say and practice.

1	2	3	4	5
6	7	8	9	10
11	12	13	14	15
16	17	18	19	20
21	22	23	24	25
26	27	28	29	30
31	32	33	34	35
36	37	38	39	40
41	42	43	44	45
46	47	48	49	50

51	52	53	54	55
56	57	58	59	60
61	62	63	64	65
66	67	68	69	70
71	72	73	74	75
76	77	78	79	80
81	82	83	84	85
86	87	88	89	90
91	92	93	94	95
96	97	98	99	100

8: ADDRESS

Listen to the teacher.

Practice with the teacher.

Read. Fill in. Copy.

ADDRESS   A __ __ R E __ __   _____

address   a __ __ r e __ __   _____

READ. FILL IN. COPY.

Circle STREET.

STREET	_ _ _ E E _

Street	_ _ _ e e _

APARTMENT	_ _ A R T M E N _

Apartment	_ _ _ r t m e n _

CITY	_ I T Y

City	_ i t y

Circle your state.

STATE	_ _ A _ E

State	_ _ a _ e

Lin More
Box 1545
Palatine, Il 60078

ZIP CODE __ I P __ O __ E

_____

zip code __ i p __ o __ e

_____

READING PRACTICE.
Read. Write.

1. STATE _____

2. STREET _____

3. City _____

4. Zip Code _____

5. CITY _____

6. Street _____

7. Apt. No. _____

8. Address _____

_____

9. State _____

10. APT. # _____

11. ZIP CODE _____

Read. Write. Remember.

Address:_____

        Number   Street

_____

    City   State   Zip Code

SPEAKING PRACTICE.

Practice with a student.

What's your street address?	5012 Main Street.
Do you live in an apartment?	Yes.
What's your apartment number?	2A.
What city do you live in?	Chicago.
What state do you live in?	Illinois.
What's your zip code?	61504.

Student A   **Student B**

What's your street address?   _____

What's your apartment number?   _____

What city do you live in?   _____

What state do you live in?   _____

What's your zip code?   _____

Write your answers. Remember them.

9: EMERGENCY NUMBERS

Listen to the teacher.

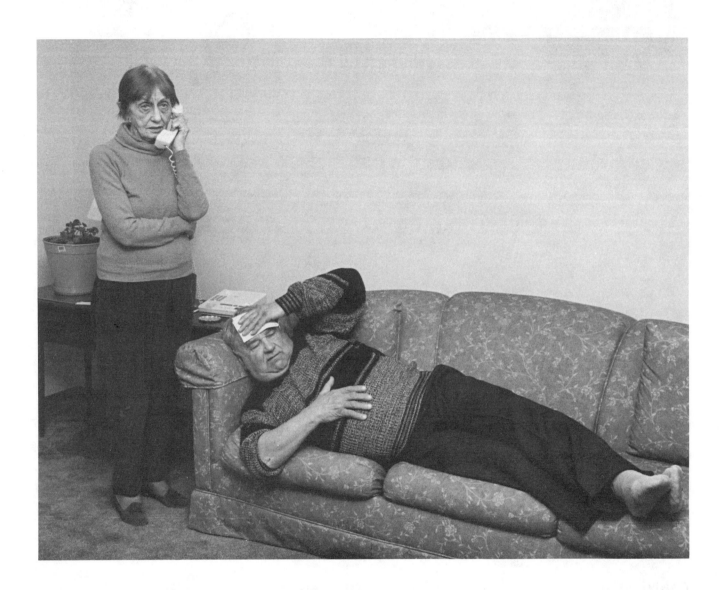

Practice with the teacher.

Read. Fill in. Copy.

EMERGENCY   __ __ E R G E __ C __   _____

emergency   __ __ e r g e __ c __   _____

READ. FILL IN. COPY.

FIRE

__ I R __

_____

POLICE

__ O L I C __

_____

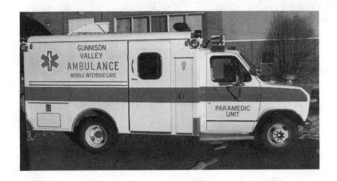

AMBULANCE

__ M B U __ A N __ __

_____

READ. WRITE. REMEMBER.
Write the phone numbers for your city.

POLICE PHONE NUMBER:	_____
FIRE PHONE NUMBER:	_____
AMBULANCE PHONE NUMBER:	_____

32

SPEAKING PRACTICE.

Practice with a student.

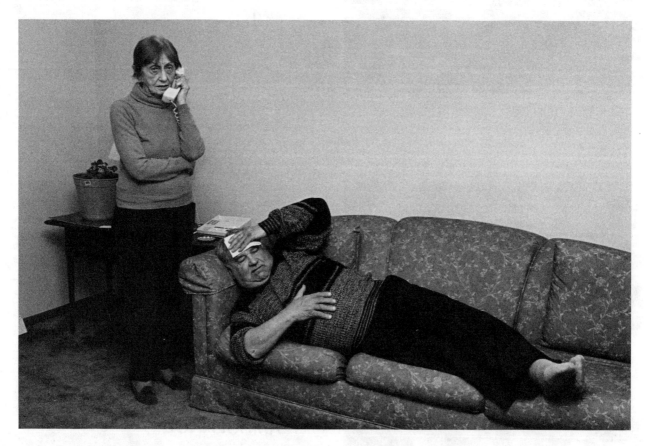

HELP! AMBULANCE! EMERGENCY!   What's your address?

453 Main Street, Apartment 3.

Student A   **Student B**

1. HELP! FIRE! EMERGENCY!   What's your address?

_____

2. HELP! POLICE! EMERGENCY!   What's your address?

_____

3. HELP! AMBULANCE! EMERGENCY!   What's your address?

_____

4. Make your own conversation.   Make your own conversation.

END OF UNIT - REVIEW

Fill out the forms.

NAME _____
          FIRST   MIDDLE   LAST

ADDRESS _____
         NUMBER   STREET

_____
            CITY   STATE   ZIP CODE

TELEPHONE NUMBER _____

SOCIAL SECURITY NUMBER _____

Name: _____

Address: _____
         No.   Street   Apt. No.

_____
        City   State   Zip Code

Soc. Sec. No: _____

Phone No: _____

10: TIMES

Read. Write the times.

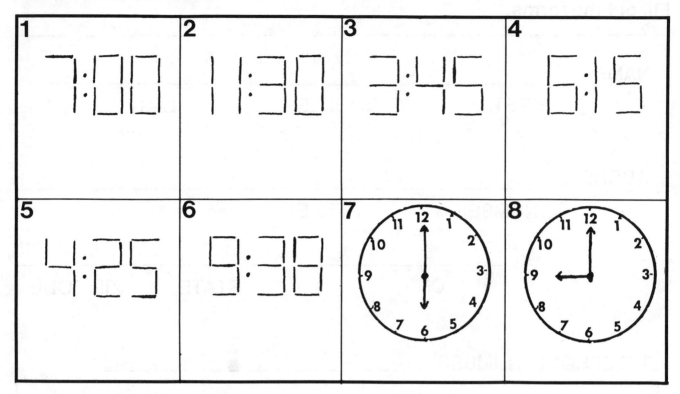

1	2	3	4
7:00	11:30	3:45	6:15

5	6	7	8
4:25	9:38		

Count and write the minutes.

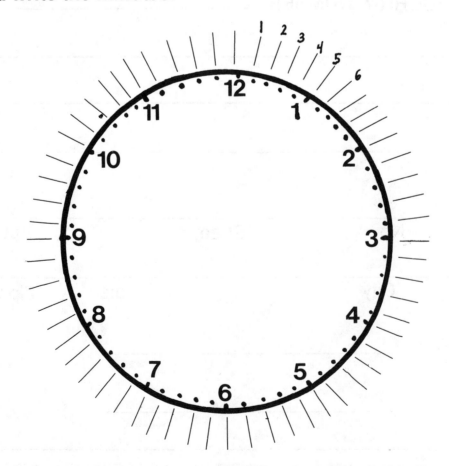

35

Read. Write the times.

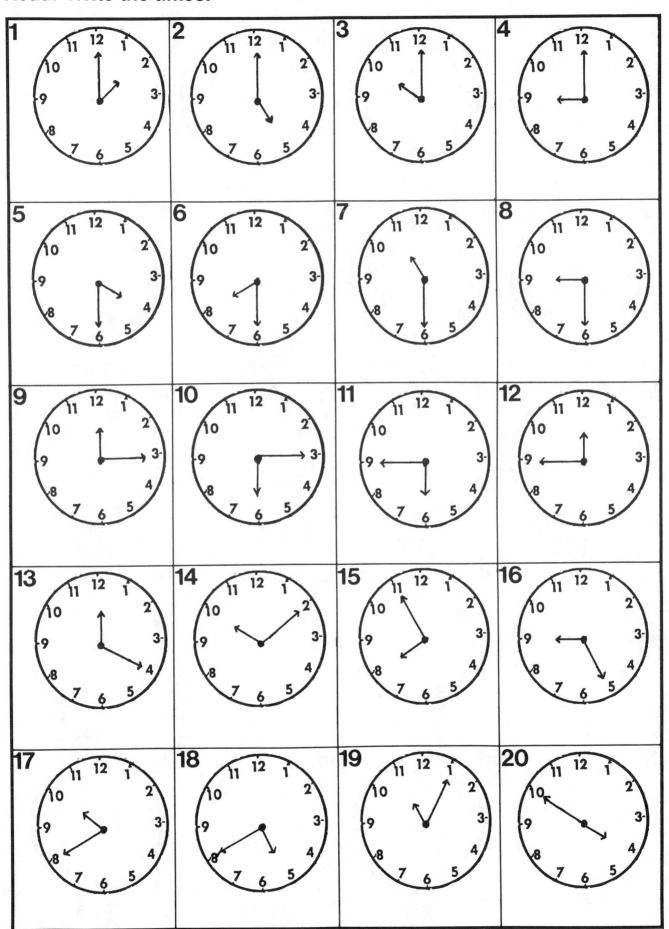

36

Read. Show the times.

1 2:00	**2** 5:00	**3** 3:30	**4** 7:30
5 12:15	**6** 10:15	**7** 7:45	**8** 3:45
9 8:20	**10** 4:05	**11** 6:25	**12** 12:55
13 2:50	**14** 11:35	**15** 2:20	**16** 9:50
17 9:15	**18** 3:45	**19** 10:10	**20** 8:55

11: DAYS OF THE WEEK

Listen to the teacher.

Practice with the teacher.

Read. Fill in. Copy.

day   __ a y   _____

week   __ __ __ k   _____

month   __ o n __ __   _____

READ. COPY.

1. SUNDAY   _____

     SUN.   _____

     S   _____

2. MONDAY   _____

     MON.   _____

     M   _____

3. TUESDAY   _____

     TUES.   _____

     T   _____

4. WEDNESDAY _____

     WED.   _____

     W   _____

5. THURSDAY _____

     THURS.   _____

     TH   _____

6. FRIDAY   _____

     FRI.   _____

     F   _____

7. SATURDAY _____

     SAT.   _____

     S   _____

LETTER AND SOUND PRACTICE.

Write the words with S.

S __ __ .

S __ __ .

Write the words with W.

w __ __ __

W __ __ .

Write the words with M.

m __ __ __ __

M __ __ .

READING PRACTICE.

Write the name of the month. Number the days.

MONTH: _____						
SUN.	MON.	TUES.	WED.	THURS.	FRI.	SAT.

Look at the calendar. Write the day.

A. 1 _____

B. 5 _____

C. 6 _____

D. 7 _____

E. 12 _____

F. 15 _____

G. 21 _____

H. 25 _____

I. 28 _____

J. 18 _____

K. 3 _____

L. 24 _____

SPEAKING PRACTICE.

Practice with a student.

Student A	**Student B**
Do you study English?	Yes.
When is your English class?	Monday through Friday from 9:00 to 11:00.
Where is your class?	In Room 2.

Student A	**Student B**
Do you study English?	_____
When is your English class?	_____
Where is your class?	_____

Write your answers. Remember them.

12: STORE SCHEDULES

Listen to the teacher.

Practice with the teacher.

Read. Fill in. Copy.

STORE   __ __ O R E   _____

store   __ __ o r e   _____

READING PRACTICE.

Say the words.

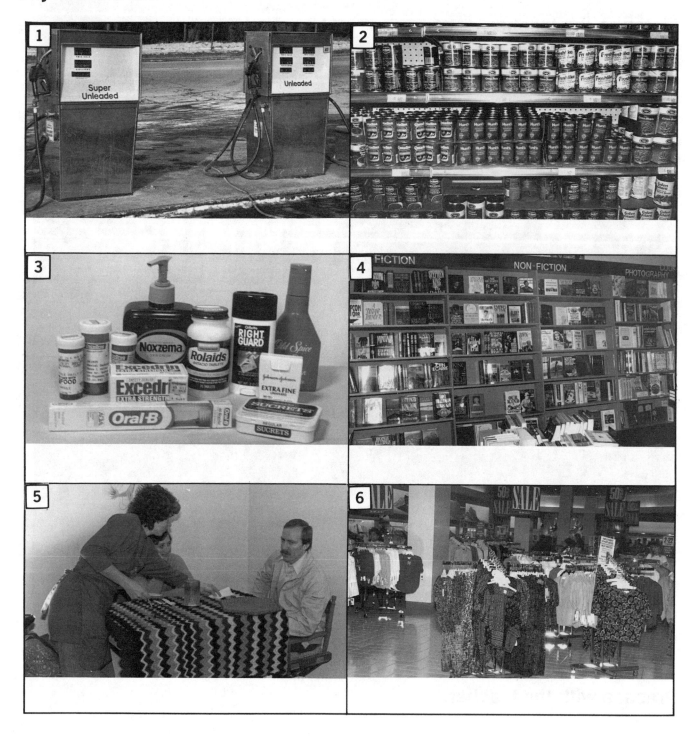

Read. Write the numbers next to the words.

_____ bookstore   _____ gas station   _____ restaurant

_____ department store   _____ pharmacy   _____ food store

Write the words under the pictures.

READ. FILL IN. COPY.

OPEN   __ P E __

CLOSED   __ __ O S E D

_____   _____

READING PRACTICE.

MAIN STREET DEPARTMENT STORE	
Sunday	Closed
Monday	9 - 9
Tuesday	9 - 5
Wednesday	9 - 5
Thursday	9 - 5
Friday	9 - 9
Saturday	9 - 9

Read.   AM = morning   PM = afternoon, night

Read. Circle OPEN or CLOSED.

1.	Monday	9:00 AM	OPEN	CLOSED
2.	Wednesday	11:00 AM	OPEN	CLOSED
3.	Saturday	3:00 PM	OPEN	CLOSED
4.	Friday	10:00 PM	OPEN	CLOSED
5.	Thursday	6:00 PM	OPEN	CLOSED
6.	Tuesday	5:30 PM	OPEN	CLOSED
7.	Monday	8:00 AM	OPEN	CLOSED
8.	Thursday	9:00 AM	OPEN	CLOSED

SPEAKING PRACTICE.
Practice with a student.

When does the <u>store</u> open?	At <u>8:30</u>.
When does it close?	At <u>12:30</u>.
Thank you.	You're welcome.

Student A

When does the _____ open?
When does it close?
Thank you.

Student B

At _____.
At _____.
You're welcome.

1. When ... department store ...?

9:00
9:00

2. When ... post office ... Sat.?

8:30
12:00

3. When ... bank ... Sat.?

9:00
1:00

4. When ... school ...?

7:00
5:00

5. Make your own conversation.

Make your own conversation.

END OF UNIT - Review

Read. Circle OPEN or CLOSED.

```
┌─────────────────────────────────┐
│       SCHOOL BOOKSTORE          │
│  Sun.            Closed         │
│  Mon.            8:00 - 9:00    │
│  Tues. - Thurs.  8:00 - 5:00    │
│  Friday          8:00 - 6:00    │
│  Sat.            9:00 - 12:00   │
└─────────────────────────────────┘
```

			OPEN	CLOSED
1.	Monday	10:00	OPEN	CLOSED
2.	Thursday	3:00	OPEN	CLOSED
3.	Saturday	5:00	OPEN	CLOSED
4.	Friday	11:30	OPEN	CLOSED
5.	Sunday	9:00	OPEN	CLOSED

```
┌─────────────────────────────────┐
│      SUSIE'S CANDY STORE        │
│        BUSINESS HOURS           │
│  Sunday thru Thursday           │
│  11:00 am - 11:00 pm    OPEN    │
│  Friday & Saturday              │
│  10:00 am - 10:00 pm            │
└─────────────────────────────────┘
```

1.	Fri.	9 AM	OPEN	CLOSED
2.	Mon.	5:30 PM	OPEN	CLOSED
3.	Wed.	1 PM	OPEN	CLOSED
4.	Thurs.	2 AM	OPEN	CLOSED
5.	Sat.	1:30 PM	OPEN	CLOSED
6.	Sun.	8:30 AM	OPEN	CLOSED

END OF UNIT - New Situation

Read. Write the telephone numbers.

```
Finberg, S 143 South St  Riverside - - - - - - - - - - - - -    233-7432
Fine, John 5467 Campbell  Riverside - - - - - - - - - - - -    233-8756
FINEST DEPARTMENT STORE  46 Main  York - - - - - -    233-6200
FIRE DEPARTMENT  756 8th  York - - - - - - - - - - - -    233-4600
Firmo, G 7353 Western  Riverside - - - - - - - - - - - - -    233-6712
FIRST NATIONAL BANK  9785 7th  York - - - - - - - - -    233-2000
FIRST STATE BANK  5243 Lincoln York - - - - - - - - -    233-7350
FIRST STREET FOOD STORE  101 First York - - - - - -    233-6000
Frank, Mary 826 Maple  Springfield - - - - - - - - - - - -    233-5436
Frank's Gas Station  701 Summit  York - - - - - - - - -    233-1902
```

1. First State Bank   _____

2. Frank's Gas Station   _____

3. Fire Department   _____

4. First Street Food Store   _____

5. Finest Department Store   _____

6. Mary Frank   _____

Read. Write.

```
         Linmore Bookstore
         HELP WANTED
           Part-time
        M  W  F  4:00 - 6:00
         Call 555-6352!
```

1. Number of days per week: _____

2. Number of hours per day: _____

3. Number of hours per week: _____

4. Phone number: _____

5. Name of store: _____

END OF UNIT - Find The Information.

Work with another student. Circle the words you know.

WASHINGTON HIGH SCHOOL
413 S. California St
Winston, IL 60651
(708) 555-7400

Class Schedule

Student's Name: _Miguel Vasquez_

Period	Time	Subject	Teacher	Room
1st period	8:00 - 8:50	ESL	Smith	101
2nd period	9:00 - 9:50	Math	Kelly	305
3rd period	10:00 -10:50	Gym	Hermann	Gym
4th period	11:00 -11:50	Science	Walsh	107
5th period	12:00 -12:50	Lunch	—	Cafeteria
6th period	1:00 - 1:50	History	Lopez	224
7th period	2:00 - 2:50	Government	Lopez	224

Circle the words and names you know.

Ace Lighting Company
WORK SCHEDULE

Week of: July 10

Day Shift
7:00 - 3:00

Department A:	Brown, Lim, Raj, Strinko, Jankowitz
Department B:	Diaz, Ramirez, Ortega, Washington
Department C:	Kang, Stern

Afternoon Shift
3:00 - 11:00

Department A:	Pao, Michalski, Lee, Chan, Petersen
Department B:	Schultz, Garcia, Vang
Department C:	Ayana

Night Shift
11:00 - 7:00

Department A:	Sanchez, Lopez, Nguyen, Riley, Duong
Department B:	Mattavongsy, Rivera, Young
Department C:	Medina

13: MONEY

READ.

penny $.01 1¢	nickel $.05 5¢	dime $.10 10¢
quarter $.25 25¢	half dollar $.50 50¢	dollar $1.00

Count. Write.

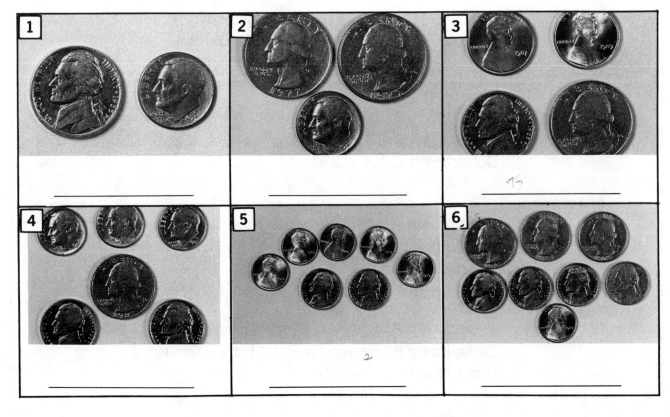

Count. Write.

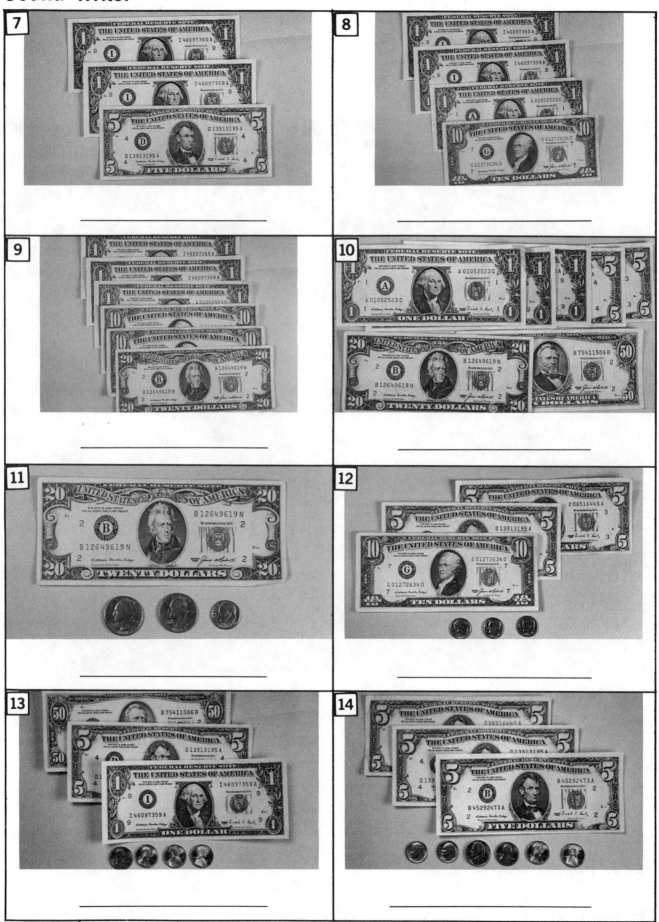

7. _____

8. _____

9. _____

10. _____

11. _____

12. _____

13. _____

14. _____

14: CHECK OUT

Listen to the teacher.

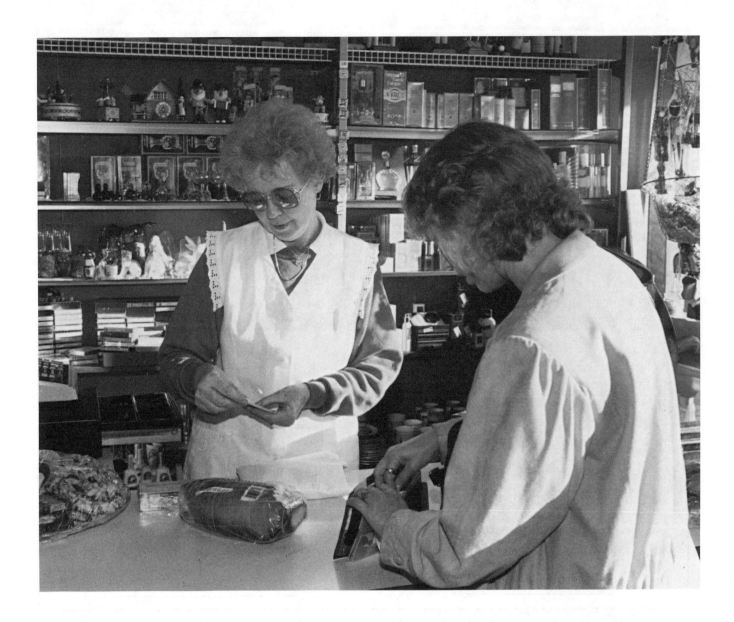

Practice with the teacher.

Read. Fill in. Copy.

CHECK OUT   C __ E C __   O U __   _____

Circle TOTAL. Circle CHANGE.

```
11/23/89  2:22PM
   CUST 239 REG  2 OPR     106
                .
GREETING CARD        1.10 TX
      FLORAL         9.99 TX
         TOTAL  $   11.87
         CASH TEND  12.00

      SUBTOTAL      11.09
      TAX PAID        .78

      13 CHANGE

         HAPPY HOLIDAYS
```

READ. COPY.

TOTAL _____

Total _____

CHANGE _____

Change _____

READING PRACTICE.

Circle the TOTAL and the CHANGE. Write.

1.
```
12-09-89    #1

PLU072       2.99 T
CTY.TAX      0.04
FOOD         0.49 T
TAX          0.22
TOTAL        3.74
CATEND       5.00
CHANGE       1.26
```

TOTAL _____

CHANGE _____

2.
```
   MARK
   10-02-89     08:58:35

---------------------------
    CUSTOMER RECEIPT
---------------------------
110 P O METER        1.65
390 POSTAGE           .25
                   --------
         TOTAL       1.90
         CASH T      2.00
                   --------
         CHANGE       .10

---------------------------

      THANK YOU
---------------------------
```

TOTAL _____

CHANGE _____

3.

```
        RESTAURANT
# 1
    1 SCR EG B    $   1.95@
      SAUSAGE     $   0.00
    1   DECAFF    $   0.60@
    1 MILK        $   0.59@
        SUB-TOTAL $   3.14
        SUB-TOTAL $   3.14
        TAX       $   0.20
    4   TOTAL     $   3.34

      AMT TEND    $  20.00
      CHANGE      $  16.66

   YOUR ORDER # IS  71
 TIME  7:19  DATE 11/04/89
    29    DINE          71
```

Total _____

Change _____

4.

```
.66lb @1.29/lbSPINA    .85
     NUTRI-GRAIN      2.92
.58lb @1.99/lbCHOC    1.15
     TAX DUE)         .10
     TOTAL           5.02
     CSH TENDER 10.02
     CHG DUE          5.00
11/22/89 16:04  0080/ 3
THANKS..YOU MAKE OUR DAY
```

Total _____

Change _____

5.

```
   12/15/89 04:54P
    8.647G @1.019
N/L  P2     8.81
TL          8.81
CASH        9.01
CNG         0.20
```

Total _____

Change _____

6.

```
12-15-89

1     $0.59
1     $0.59
1     $0.59
      $1.77  ST
     $0.04 TX 1

      $1.81  TL
   $10.01 CA
     $8.20  CG

   10-44
 94390001
```

Total _____

Change _____

SPEAKING PRACTICE.

Practice with a student.

Cashier

Customer

That's $10.00.

Here's your change, $10.00.

Have a nice day.

Here's $20.00.

Thank you.

Student A

That's $_____.

Here's your change, $_____.

Have a nice day.

Student B

Here's $_____.

Thank you.

1. That's $4.75
   $.25

   $5.00

2. That's $17.75.
   $2.25

   $20.00

3. That's $32.50.
   $17.50

   $50.00

4. That's $.75.
   $4.25

   $5.00

5. Make your own conversation.

   Make your own conversation.

15: CLOTHES

Listen to the teacher.

RETURNS

HERE

Practice with the teacher.

Write the names of clothing stores in your city.

_____

_____

_____

READING PRACTICE.

Say the words.

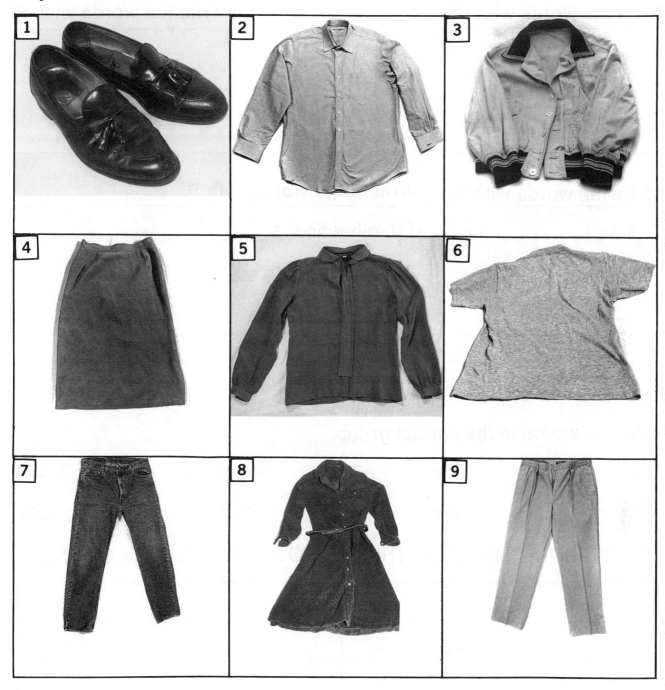

Read. Write the numbers next to the words.

_____ dress   _____ shoes   _____ blouse   _____ skirt

_____ slacks   _____ shirt   _____ jacket   _____ T shirt

_____ jeans

Write the words under the pictures.

56

LETTER AND SOUND PRACTICE.

Write the words with SH.

sh __ __ __

__ sh __ __ __

sh __ __ __

Write the words with J.

j __ __ __ __

j __ __ __ __ __

Write the words with S.

s __ __ __ __

s __ __ __ __ __

__ __ __ ss

Write other words with S.

1. brother and s __ __ __ __ __

2. food s __ __ __ __

3. gas s __ __ __ __ __ __

READING PRACTICE.

Write the words in the correct group.

dress   jeans   shoes   T shirt

blouse   shirt   jacket   slacks

GIRLS' AND WOMEN'S CLOTHING   BOYS' AND MEN'S CLOTHING

Read the sizes.

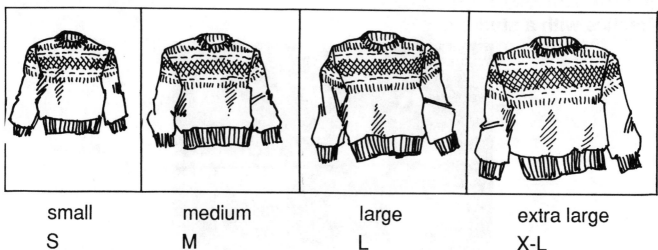

small	medium	large	extra large
S	M	L	X-L

Read. Write the size. Write the price.

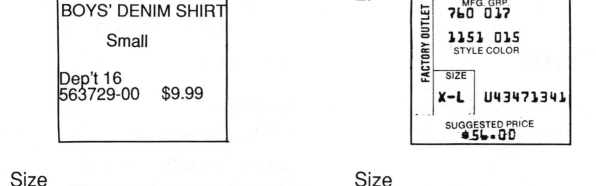

1.

BOYS' DENIM SHIRT

Small

Dep't 16
563729-00 $9.99

2.

12665
MFG. GRP.
760 017

1151 015
STYLE COLOR

FACTORY OUTLET

SIZE
X-L   U43471341

SUGGESTED PRICE
$56.00

Size _____

Price _____

Size _____

Price _____

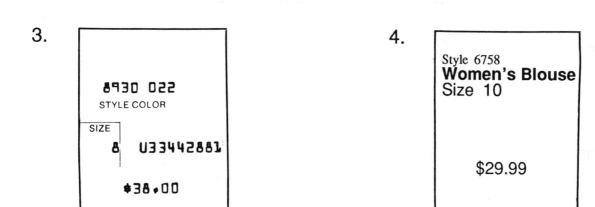

3.

8930 022
STYLE COLOR

SIZE
8   U33442881

$38.00

4.

Style 6758
Women's Blouse
Size 10

$29.99

Size _____

Price _____

Size _____

Price _____

SPEAKING PRACTICE.

Practice with a student.

I'd like to return <u>this blouse.</u>

It's <u>too big.</u>

Yes. Here it is.

<u>A refund,</u> please.

What's the problem?

Do you have the receipt?

Do you want to exchange it or do you want a refund?

Here you are.

Student A

I'd like to return _____.

It's _____.

Yes. Here it is.

_____, please.

Student B

What's the problem?

Do you have the receipt?

Do you want to exchange it or do you want a refund?

Here you are.

1. this dress
   too big
   a refund

2. this shirt
   too small
   Exchange it

3. these shoes
   too big
   A refund

4. Make your own conversation.

Make your own conversation.

59

16: BUYING FOOD

Listen to the teacher.

Practice with the teacher.

Write the names of food stores in your city.

_____

_____

_____

READING PRACTICE.

Say the words.

Read. Write the numbers next to the words.

____ apples   ____ bananas   ____ oranges   ____ grapes

____ carrots   ____ potatoes   ____ tomatoes   ____ onions

____ green beans

Write the words under the pictures.

READING PRACTICE.

Say the words.

Read. Write the number next to the word.

_____ ground beef	_____ chicken	_____ fish	_____ steak
_____ milk	_____ eggs	_____ juice	_____ rice
_____ cheese			

Write the words under the pictures.

LETTER AND SOUND PRACTICE.

Write the words with B.

b __ __ __ __ __ __

b __ __ __

b __ __ __ __

Write the words with CH.

ch __ __ __ __

ch __ __ __ __ __

READ. FILL IN. COPY.

ounce __ __ n c e

oz. __ __.

dozen __ o z e __

doz. __ o __.

half gallon __ a l f __ a l l o __

half gal. __ a l f __ __.

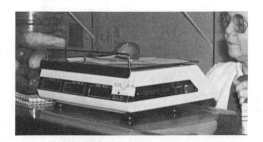

pound __ __ __ n d

lb. __ __.

quart __ __ a r t

qt. __ __.

gallon __ a __ __ o n

gal. __ __ __.

63

WRITE. REMEMBER.

_____ ounces = 1 pound

_____ quarts = 1 gallon

_____ = 1 dozen

READING PRACTICE.
Read and write.

1.

```
       SLICED  BEEF

USDA INSPECTED
  NET WT./COUNT     UNIT PRICE      TOTAL PRICE
    0.62 lb        $0.98        $  0.61

    201772 900615
```

Weight _____

Total Price _____

2.

```
           GROUND  BEEF

  NET WT./COUNT    UNIT PRICE      TOTAL PRICE
     1.14 lb       $1.89        $2.15

    01655 002153
```

Weight _____

Total Price _____

3.

```
    05786  203762
       ROAST  BEEF

  | NET WT/CT | UNIT PRICE |  TOTAL PRICE
     0.65lb      5.78        $3.76
```

Weight _____

Total Price _____

4.

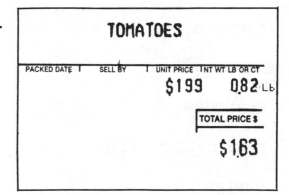

```
         TOMATOES

PACKED DATE |   SELL BY   | UNIT PRICE  NT WT LB OR CT
                            $199     0.82 Lb

                        TOTAL PRICE $
                            $1.63
```

Weight _____

Total Price _____

READING PRACTICE.

Read.

 STAR FOOD MART
2500 Main Street
556-7000

FRUIT and VEGETABLES		MEAT	
Apples	59 ¢ lb.	Ground Beef	$1.19 lb.
Potatoes	19 ¢ lb.	Chicken	50 ¢ lb.
Onions	10 ¢ lb.		
		DAIRY	
Tomatoes	49 ¢ lb.	Large Eggs	89 ¢ doz.
Grapes	89 ¢ lb.	Milk	$1.99 gal.
Bananas	29 ¢ lb.	Ice Cream	$1.49 quart

Write the prices.

1. 1 pound of apples _____

2. 1 gallon of milk _____

3. 1 dozen eggs _____

4. 1 pound of ground beef _____

5. 1 pound of potatoes _____

6. 1 pound of bananas _____

7. 1 pound of grapes _____

8. 1 pound of onions _____

Count. Write the prices.

1. 2 lbs. of apples _____

2. 5 lbs. onions _____

3. 3 doz. eggs _____

4. 2 gals. of milk _____

5. 4 lbs. of ground beef _____

6. 10 lbs. of potatoes _____

7. 2 qts. of ice cream _____

8. 2 lbs. of bananas _____

SPEAKING PRACTICE.
Practice with a student.

Customer	Clerk

I'd like <u>two pounds of sausage</u>.

<u>Two pounds at $1.49 a pound.</u>
That's <u>$2.98.</u>

Thank you.

You're welcome.

Student A

I'd like _____.

Thank you.

Student B

_____.

That's _____.

You're welcome.

1. one pound of ground beef

One pound at $1.99 a pound.
$1.99

2. one half pound of roast beef

One half pound at $3.58 a pound
$1.79.

3. two pounds of ham

Two pounds at $1.69 a pound.
$3.38

4. Make your own conversation.

Make your own conversation.

66

SPEAKING PRACTICE.

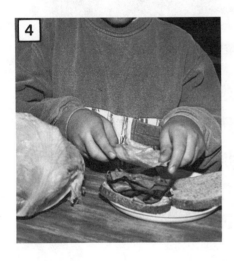  

Say the instructions.

READING PRACTICE.

Read and do.

I Make My Lunch For School

1. Take 2 pieces of bread.

2. Put some butter on the bread.

3. Put some roast beef on the bread.

4. Put some lettuce on the roast beef.

5. Put the sandwich in a plastic bag.

6. Put the sandwich in a paper bag.

7. Put some potato chips in the paper bag.

8. Put an apple in the paper bag.

9. Close the bag.

Read and write.

1. Take 2 pieces of b __ __ __ __.

2. Put some butter on the bread.

3. Put some roast beef on the b __ __ __ __.

4. Put some lettuce on the roast b __ __ __.

5. Put the sandwich in a p __ __ __ __ __ __ bag.

6. Put the sandwich in a p __ __ __ __ bag.

7. Put some p __ __ __ __ __ chips in the paper bag.

8. P __ __ an apple in the paper bag.

9. Close the b __ __.

17: FAST FOOD RESTAURANTS

Listen to the teacher.

Practice with the teacher.

Write the names of fast food restaurants in your city.

_____

_____

_____

READING PRACTICE.

Say the words.

Read. Write the numbers next to the words.

_____ hamburger   _____ French fries   _____ fish sandwich   _____ tea

_____ cheeseburger   _____ hot dog   _____ pizza   _____ taco

_____ coffee

Write the words under the pictures.

70

LETTER AND SOUND PRACTICE.

Write the words with F.

```
f __ __ __

F __ __ __ __ __    F __ __ __ __
```

Write the words with H.

```
h __ __ __ __ __

h __ __ __ __ __ __ __
```

Write the words with CH.

```
        ch __ __ __ __

        __ __ __ __ __ __ ch
```

Write the words with T.

```
    t __ __ __

    t __ __
```

READING PRACTICE.

Read the words.

cheeseburger	milk	tea	hamburger
taco	hot dog	chicken	coffee

Write the words in the correct group.

Food	Drinks

SPEAKING PRACTICE.
Practice with a student.

Clerk

Customer

Can I help you?

I'd like a hamburger and a Pepsi.

That's $2.60.

Here you are.

Thank you. Come again.

Good-bye.

Student A

Student B

Can I help you?

I'd like _____.

That's _____.

Here you are.

Thank you. Come again.

Good-bye.

1. Can ...?
   $3.24

2 hamburgers, 1 small Coke

2. Can ...?
   $2.93

1 hot dog, 1 small fries, 1 coffee

3. Can ...?
   $2.50

2 tacos, 1 small milk

4. Make your own conversation.

Make your own conversation.

READING PRACTICE.

Read.

```
┌─────────────────────────────────────────────┐
│              FAST FOOD MENU                   │
│                                               │
│   Taco                  .75                   │
│   Hamburger            1.30                   │
│   Cheeseburger         1.60                   │
│   Hot Dog               .90                   │
│   Fish                 1.50                   │
│   French Fries      Sm. .50    Lrg. .80       │
│   Coke, Pepsi, 7-Up Sm. .50    Lrg. .95       │
│   Milk              Sm. .50    Lrg. .75       │
│   Coffee            Sm. .45    Lrg. .70       │
└─────────────────────────────────────────────┘
```

Write the prices. Write the total.

1. 1 hot dog   _____   2. 1 hamburger   _____

    1 small French Fries   _____   1 small milk   _____

    1 small Coke   _____   1 large coffee   _____

           TOTAL: _____   TOTAL: _____

3. 2 fish sandwiches   _____   4. Write your own order.

    1 hot dog   _____   _____

    1 hamburger   _____   _____

    2 small fries   _____   _____

    1 small milk   _____   _____

    1 small coffee   _____   _____

                                            _____

           TOTAL: _____   TOTAL: _____

73

END OF UNIT - Review

Write. Read.

1.

12 08 MMHGI

Boy's Jeans
Size 10

0911 $15.99

Name of clothing: _____

Size: _____

Price: _____

2.

0 209407 003472

ROAST BEEF

UNIT PRICE $

5.78   12 10 89

0.60   **3.47**
WEIGHT   TOTAL PRICE $

Name of food: _____

Weight: _____

Total Price: _____

3.

GREEN BEANS

PACKED DATE   SELL BY   UNIT PRICE   NT WT LB OR CT

$1.29   0.81

TOTAL PRICE $

204100 001046   04100 $1.04

CODE

PRODUCE

Name of food: _____

Weight: _____

Total Price: _____

4.

No. ELD 1-12-91
STYLE T.shirt
SIZE SM
PRICE 6.50

Name of clothing: _____

Size: _____

Price: _____

Read.

Bananas
39¢
lb.

Ruby Red
Seedless Grapes
98¢
lb.

Yellow Onions
3 lb. bag # 69¢ ea.

Crispy, Crunchy
California Carrots
2 # 49¢
lb. Bag

Large Size Idaho
Baking Potatoes
49¢
lb.

U.S. No. 1, Extra Fancy, Washington State
Red or Golden Delicious Apples
per lb. # 39¢

Whole Frying Chickens
39¢
(limit 3)
lb.

Green Beans .... # 79¢ lb.

5 lb. pkg. or more
75% Lean Ground Beef ....
$1 39 lb.
Less than 5 lb. pkg. $1.49 lb.

Large Eggs
59¢
One Dozen

3.38 lb.
Wisconsin American Cheese
1 69
½ lb.

Read the ads on page 75. Write the prices.

1. 1 lb. of bananas _____
2. 1 bag of carrots _____
3. 1 lb. of potatoes _____
4. 1/2 lb. of cheese _____
5. 1 bag of onions _____
6. 1 lb. of green beans _____

7. 1 lb. of grapes _____
8. 1 lb. of red apples _____
9. 1 dozen eggs _____
10. 3 lbs. of onions _____
11. 12 eggs _____
12. 2 lbs. of carrots _____

Write the prices. Read.

1. 2 bags of carrots _____
2. 3 bags of onions _____
3. 5 lbs. of potatoes _____
4. a 4 lb. chicken _____
5. 6 lbs. of ground beef _____
6. 2 lbs. of ground beef _____
7. 1 lb. of cheese _____
8. 3 dozen eggs _____

9. 2 lbs. of ground beef _____
10. a 3 lb. chicken _____
11. 2 dozen eggs _____
12. 5 bags of carrots _____
13. 7 lbs. of bananas _____
14. 10 lbs. of potatoes _____
15. 5 lbs. of red apples _____
16. 2 lbs. of cheese _____

Make a shopping list. Write the prices.

_____

_____

_____

_____

END OF UNIT - New Situation

Write. Read.

Price of 1 package of sausage links _____   Price of 1 dozen eggs _____

Price of a 10 pound turkey _____   Price of a 20 pound turkey _____

Purchase Any...

Color Television

$219

TAKE AN ADDITIONAL...

$20⁰⁰ OFF

½ gal.

Ice Cream

Vanilla FLAVORED Ice Cream

Chocolate Ice Cream

2/$3

Regular price of a color TV _____   Price of a 1/2 gal. of ice cream _____

Sale price of a color TV _____   Price of 1 gal. of ice cream _____

77

Work with another student. Circle the words you know.

NEW FASHION CLOTHING STORE
137 N. Cumberland Ave.
Maybrook
556-7350

SAVE 50% TO 70%
ON OUR ENTIRE INVENTORY!

Shoes, Boots & Handbags

$25 OFF SALE PRICE! Men's & Women's Winter Coats
Priced $79.99 to $99.99

$20 OFF SALE PRICE! Men's & Boys' Suits
Priced $54.99 to $74.99

$15 OFF SALE PRICE! Women's Silk Evening Dresses
Priced $39.99 to $49.99

$10 OFF SALE PRICE! Men's & Boys' 100% Wool Slacks
Priced $24.99 to $34.99

SATISFACTION GUARANTEED
Or Your Money Back

**HOURS: MON.- FRI. 8 a.m. - 10 p.m.
SAT. 8 a.m. - 9 p.m.
SUN. 8 a.m. - 8 p.m.**

TOMORROW ONLY! TAKE AN EXTRA 25% OFF

18: DATES

1993			

JANUARY
S	M	T	W	TH	F	S
					1	2
3	4	5	6	7	8	9
10	11	12	13	14	15	16
17	18	19	20	21	22	23
24	25	26	27	28	29	30
31						

FEBRUARY
S	M	T	W	TH	F	S
	1	2	3	4	5	6
7	8	9	10	11	12	13
14	15	16	17	18	19	20
21	22	23	24	25	26	27
28						

MARCH
S	M	T	W	TH	F	S
	1	2	3	4	5	6
7	8	9	10	11	12	13
14	15	16	17	18	19	20
21	22	23	24	25	26	27
28	29	30	31			

APRIL
S	M	T	W	TH	F	S
				1	2	3
4	5	6	7	8	9	10
11	12	13	14	15	16	17
18	19	20	21	22	23	24
25	26	27	28	29	30	

MAY
S	M	T	W	TH	F	S
						1
2	3	4	5	6	7	8
9	10	11	12	13	14	15
16	17	18	19	20	21	22
23	24	25	26	27	28	29
30	31					

JUNE
S	M	T	W	TH	F	S
		1	2	3	4	5
6	7	8	9	10	11	12
13	14	15	16	17	18	19
20	21	22	23	24	25	26
27	28	29	30			

JULY
S	M	T	W	TH	F	S
				1	2	3
4	5	6	7	8	9	10
11	12	13	14	15	16	17
18	19	20	21	22	23	24
25	26	27	28	29	30	31

AUGUST
S	M	T	W	TH	F	S
1	2	3	4	5	6	7
8	9	10	11	12	13	14
15	16	17	18	19	20	21
22	23	24	25	26	27	28
29	30	31				

SEPTEMBER
S	M	T	W	TH	F	S
			1	2	3	4
5	6	7	8	9	10	11
12	13	14	15	16	17	18
19	20	21	22	23	24	25
26	27	28	29	30		

OCTOBER
S	M	T	W	TH	F	S
					1	2
3	4	5	6	7	8	9
10	11	12	13	14	15	16
17	18	19	20	21	22	23
24	25	26	27	28	29	30
31						

NOVEMBER
S	M	T	W	TH	F	S
	1	2	3	4	5	6
7	8	9	10	11	12	13
14	15	16	17	18	19	20
21	22	23	24	25	26	27
28	29	30				

DECEMBER
S	M	T	W	TH	F	S
			1	2	3	4
5	6	7	8	9	10	11
12	13	14	15	16	17	18
19	20	21	22	23	24	25
26	27	28	29	30	31	

READ. FILL IN. COPY.

1. January   __ a __ u a r __   _____

    Jan.   __ a __ .   _____

2. February   __ __ b r u a __ __   _____

    Feb.   __ e __ .   _____

3. March   __ a r __ __   _____

    Mar.   __ a __ .   _____

4. April   __ p r i __   _____

    Apr.   __ p r.   _____

5. May   __ a y   _____

     May   __ __ __   _____

6. June   __ u n __   _____

     June   __ __ __ __   _____

7. July   __ u l __   _____

     July   __ __ __ __   _____

8. August   __ u g u __ __   _____

     Aug.   __ u g.   _____

9. September   __ e p __ e m b __ __   _____

     Sept.   __ e p __.   _____

10. October   __ c t o b __ __   _____

     Oct.   __ c __.   _____

11. November   __ o v e m __ __ __   _____

     Nov.   __ o __.   _____

12. December   __ e c e m __ __ __   _____

     Dec.   __ __ c.   _____

LETTER AND SOUND PRACTICE.

Write the months with M.   **Write other words with M.**

M __ __.	father and m __ __ __ __ __
M __ __	Sunday, M __ __ __ __ __, Tuesday

Write the months with J.   **Write other words with J.**

J __ __.	T shirt and j __ __ __ __
J __ __ __	slacks, shirt, tie, and j __ __ __ __ __ __
J __ __ __	

READING PRACTICE.

Read.

1994		

Jan.

S	M	T	W	TH	F	S
						1
2	3	4	5	6	7	8
9	10	11	12	13	14	15
16	17	18	19	20	21	22
23	24	25	26	27	28	29
30	31					

Feb.

S	M	T	W	TH	F	S
		1	2	3	4	5
6	7	8	9	10	11	12
13	14	15	16	17	18	19
20	21	22	23	24	25	26
27	28					

Mar.

S	M	T	W	TH	F	S
		1	2	3	4	5
6	7	8	9	10	11	12
13	14	15	16	17	18	19
20	21	22	23	24	25	26
27	28	29	30	31		

Apr.

S	M	T	W	TH	F	S
					1	2
3	4	5	6	7	8	9
10	11	12	13	14	15	16
17	18	19	20	21	22	23
24	25	26	27	28	29	30

May

S	M	T	W	TH	F	S
1	2	3	4	5	6	7
8	9	10	11	12	13	14
15	16	17	18	19	20	21
22	23	24	25	26	27	28
29	30	31				

June

S	M	T	W	TH	F	S
			1	2	3	4
5	6	7	8	9	10	11
12	13	14	15	16	17	18
19	20	21	22	23	24	25
26	27	28	29	30		

July

S	M	T	W	TH	F	S
					1	2
3	**4**	5	6	7	8	9
10	11	12	13	14	15	16
17	18	19	20	21	22	23
24	25	26	27	28	29	30
31						

Aug.

S	M	T	W	TH	F	S
	1	2	3	4	5	6
7	8	9	10	11	12	13
14	15	16	17	18	19	20
21	22	23	24	25	26	27
28	29	30	31			

Sept.

S	M	T	W	TH	F	S
				1	2	3
4	5	6	7	8	9	10
11	12	13	14	15	16	17
18	19	20	21	22	23	24
25	26	27	28	29	30	

Oct.

S	M	T	W	TH	F	S
						1
2	3	4	5	6	7	8
9	10	11	12	13	14	15
16	17	18	19	20	21	22
23	24	25	26	27	28	29
30	31					

Nov.

S	M	T	W	TH	F	S
		1	2	3	4	5
6	7	8	9	10	11	12
13	14	15	16	17	18	19
20	21	22	23	**24**	25	26
27	28	29	30			

Dec.

S	M	T	W	TH	F	S
				1	2	3
4	5	6	7	8	9	10
11	12	13	14	15	16	17
18	19	20	21	22	23	**24**
25	26	27	28	29	30	**31**

READ.

Sunday   Monday   Tuesday   Wednesday

Thursday   Friday   Saturday

Circle these dates on page 81. Write the day.

1.   Jan. 10, 1994   _____

2.   Nov. 23, 1994   _____

3.   Dec. 3, 1994   _____

4.   Mar. 1, 1994   _____

5.   June 9, 1994   _____

6.   Apr. 15, 1994   _____

7.   Feb. 28, 1994   _____

8.   Aug. 21, 1994   _____

9.   May 27, 1994   _____

10. June 5, 1994   _____

Write the dates and days for the holidays.

	Date	Day
1. New Year's Day	_____	_____
2. Christmas	_____	_____
3. Thanksgiving	_____	_____
4. Christmas Eve	_____	_____
5. New Year's Eve	_____	_____
6. Independence Day	_____	_____

19: PERSONAL DATES

Listen to the teacher.

Practice with the teacher.

Read. Fill in. Copy.

birthday   __ i r __ __ __ __ __   _____

age   __ g e   _____

Circle BIRTH DATE, BIRTHPLACE, and DATE OF ENTRY.

Name: _____

Address: _____

_____

Phone No.: _____ Soc. Sec. No.:_____

Birth date: _____ Birthplace: _____

Date of entry: _____

READING PRACTICE.

Write about you.

1. Birthday _____

2. Birth date _____

3. Birthplace _____

4. Date of entry in the U.S. _____

5. Date of birth _____

6. Age _____

READ. WRITE. REMEMBER.

Birthplace _____

Date of birth _____

Age _____

Date of entry in the U.S. _____

SPEAKING PRACTICE.
Practice with a student.

My name is Thavisouk Mattavongsy.

Pleased to meet you, too.

Pleased to meet you.

My name is Ann Snow.

Please sit down.

I'd like to ask you some questions.

Ann's Questions	Thavisouk's Answers
How old are you?	25.
What is your birth date?	December 29, 1964.
When did you come to the U.S.?	April 25, 1983.

Student A

How old are you?

What is your birth date?

When did you come to the U.S.?

Student B

_____

_____

_____

Write your answers on the lines. Remember them.

20: DOCTOR'S APPOINTMENTS

Listen to the teacher.

Practice with the teacher.

Read. Fill in. Copy.

doctor   __ o c t o r   _____

appointment   a __ __ o i n t __ __ __ __   _____

READING PRACTICE.
Say the words.

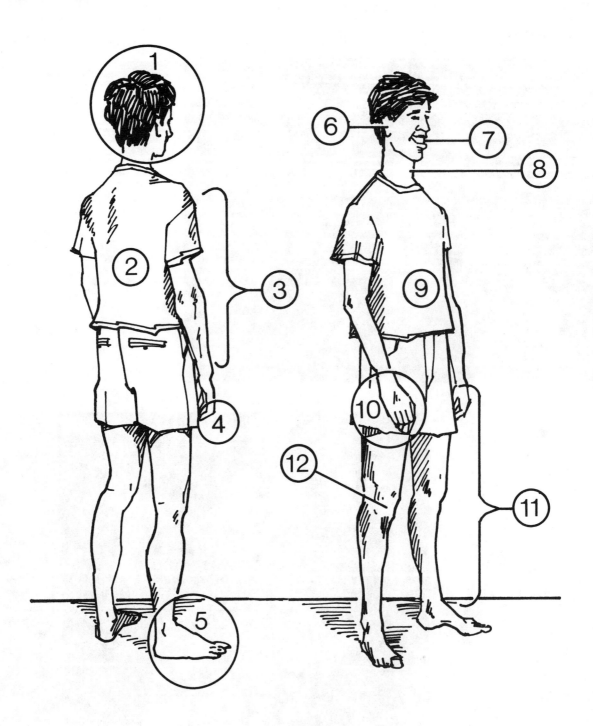

Read. Write the numbers next to the words.

____ head		____ ear		____ back		____ stomach
____ throat		____ leg		____ tooth		____ knee
____ arm		____ foot		____ hand		____ finger

READ.

ache	sore	broken
earache	sore throat	broken finger
backache	sore arm	broken hand
stomachache	sore knee	broken foot
toothache		broken leg

SOUND AND LETTER PRACTICE.

Write the words with S.

s __ __ __

s __ __ __ __ __ __

Write other words with S.

s __ __ __ __ or large

Fri., S __ __ ., S __ __ .

S __ __ . S __ __ . #

Write the words with TH.

th __ __ __ __

__ __ __ th

Write other words with TH.

Wed., Th __ __ __ ., Fri.

12 __ __ __ ths in a year

Write the words with H.

h __ __ __

h __ __ __

Write other words with H.

H __ __ __   WANTED

Can I h __ __ __ you?

Write the words with B.

b __ __ __

b __ __ __ __ __

b __ __ __ __ __ __ __

Write other words with B.

green b __ __ __ __

ground b __ __ __

sister and b __ __ __ __ __ __

Read. Write.

1.

For *Carmen Lopez*

Date: *Sept. 28*

Time: *9:00*

Dr. Mary Smith
305 W. North Ave. Columbus
555-4615

Dr.'s Name: _____

Appointment Date: _____

Appointment Time: _____

2.

Dr. Miller
341 Summit Street
555-3826

Your next visit is scheduled for:

10 AM on July 9

Dr.'s Name: _____

Appointment Date: _____

Appointment Time: _____

3.

APPOINTMENT
Your next appointment is on

Feb. 10 at *2:15*

Dr. Maria Harris
3415 Main St.   San Diego
555-3725

Please cancel at least 24 hours in advance if you are unable to make your appointment.

Dr.'s Name: _____

Appointment Time: _____

Appointment Date: _____

READ. WRITE. REMEMBER.

Doctor's Name: _____

Dentist's Name: _____

Name of hospital: _____

SPEAKING PRACTICE.
Practice with a student.

I'd like to make an appointment.

I have <u>a sore throat</u>.

<u>At 2:00. Yes.</u>

<u>Irma Sanchez.</u>

Thank you.

What's the matter?

Can you come <u>at 2:00</u>?

What's your name?

See you <u>at 2:00</u> Mrs. Sanchez.

Good-bye.

Student A

I'd like to make an appointment.

I have _____.

_____ Yes.

_____.

Thank you.

1. a stomachache
2. a fever
3. a toothache
4. Make your own conversation.

Student B

What's the matter?

Can you come _____?

What's your name?

See you _____.

Good-bye.

at 4:00

at 9:00 tomorrow morning

next Wed., at 10:00

Make your own conversation.

Read and say.

I'd like to make an appointment.

No, I'm busy.

Yes. Monday at 9:00.

Can you come today at 3:00?

Can you come at 9:00 on Monday?

Thank you. Good-bye.

90

SPEAKING PRACTICE.

Listen to your teacher.

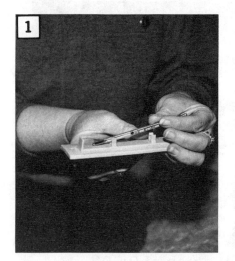 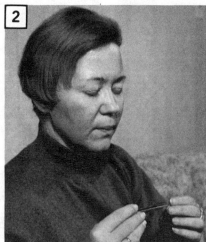 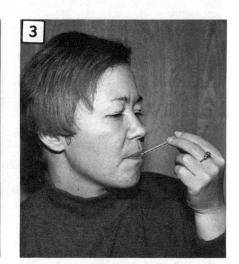

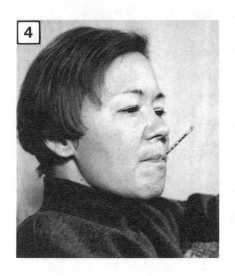 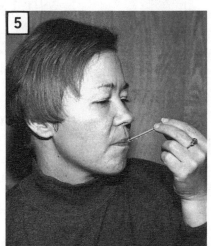 

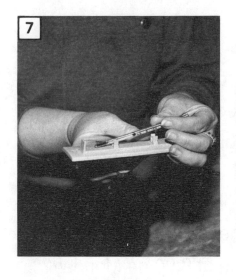  

Say the instructions.

READING PRACTICE.

Read and do.

1. Take out the thermometer.

2. Check it.

3. Put the thermometer in your mouth.

4. Wait 1 minute.

5. Take the thermometer out of your mouth.

6. Read it.

7. Put away the thermometer.

8. If you have a slight fever, take some medicine.

9. If you have a high fever, call a doctor.

Read and write.

1. T __ __ __ out the thermometer.

2. Ch __ __ __ it.

3. Put the thermometer in your m __ __ __ __.

4. Wait 1 m __ __ __ __ __.

5. T __ __ __ the thermometer out of your mouth.

6. R __ __ __ it.

7. P __ __ away the thermometer.

8. If you have a slight fever, t __ __ __ some medicine.

9. If you have a high fever, call a d __ __ __ __ __.

21: BILLS

Listen to the teacher.

Practice with the teacher.

Read. Fill in. Copy.

bill   __ i __ __   _____

READ. FILL IN. COPY.

water

__ a __ e r

_____

electricity

__ l e c t r i __ __ __ __

_____

gas

__ a s

_____

Circle AMOUNT DUE. Underline DATE DUE.

PHONE BILL		
	SUMMARY	
Current Charges	Illinois Bell	44.06
Payments and Adjustments	Previous Bill	58.89
	Payment/s Received	-58.89
	Current Charges	44.06
	Total Amount Due	44.06
	Date Due	NOV 22, 1989

AMOUNT DUE

__ __ O U __ T __ U E

_____

DATE DUE

__ __ __ __   D __ __

_____

READING PRACTICE.

Circle the amount due. Underline the date due. Write.

ELECTRIC BILL

RESIDENTIAL SERVICE - METER D254970
PRESENT REGULAR   READING   98523

      TOTAL KILOWATTHOURS (KWH) USED   857
      CUSTOMER CHARGE (SINGLE DWELLING) $ 11.24
ENERGY CHARGE: 1ST 400 KWH X $.09208   36.83
              REMAINING 457 KWH X .04627   21.15
   ELECTRIC ADJUST   857 KWH X -.00088   -.75

      BULB SERVICE   500 KWH X .00184   .92
       STATE TAX   857 KWH X .00320 ~ 2.74
   REGULATORY TAX $ 69.39 X 0.100%   .07
      AMOUNT DUE (29 DAYS OF SERVICE) $ 72.20

ACCOUNT
NUMBER   21629424100

DUE 12-07-89

Water Bill

SERVICE AT ADDRESS BELOW

409 SOUTH ST

PREVIOUS READING	PRESENT READING	USAGE THOUSAND GALLONS
590	605	15

WATER

31.92

NOW DUE ►   31.92

DATE DUE   10/19/89

RETAIN THIS PORTION FOR YOUR RECORDS

ACCT. #
   785004090000

Bill: _____

Amount Due:_____

Date Due: _____

Bill: _____

Amount Due: _____

Date Due: _____

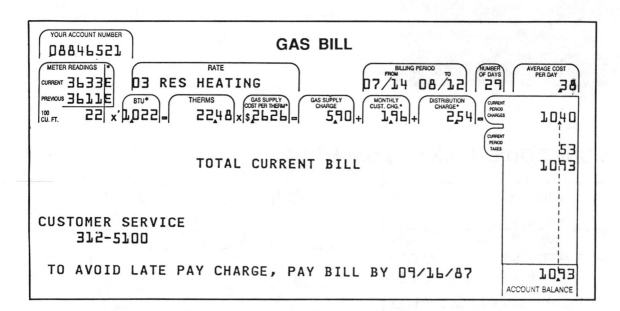

Bill: _____

Date Due: _____

Amount Due:_____

SPEAKING PRACTICE.
Practice with a student.

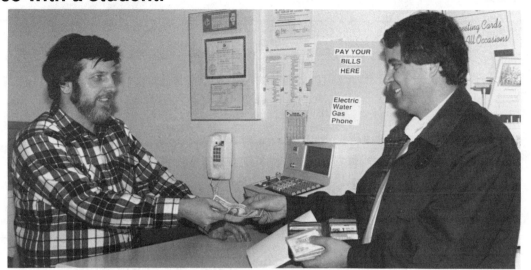

Clerk	Customer
Can I help you?	I'd like to pay my phone bill.
It's $35.00.	Here's $40.00.
Your change is $5.00.	Thank you.

Student A

Can I help you?

It's _____.

Your change is _____.

Student B

I'd like to pay my _____.

Here's _____.

Thank you.

Student A	Student B
1. Can ...? $18.50 $1.50	gas bill $20.00
2. Can ...? $73.89 $6.11	electric bill $80.00
3. Can ...? $45.00 $5.00	doctor's bill $50.00
4. Make your own conversation.	Make your own conversation.

END OF UNIT - Review

Read. Write.

Name _____

       First   Middle   Last

Address _____

       #   Street

_____

      City   State   Zip Code

Phone Number (_____) _____

Age _____   Birth date _____

Birthplace _____

Names, birth dates, and ages of family members:

Names	Relationship	Birth dates	Ages
_____	_____	_____	_____
_____	_____	_____	_____
_____	_____	_____	_____
_____	_____	_____	_____
_____	_____	_____	_____
_____	_____	_____	_____
_____	_____	_____	_____
_____	_____	_____	_____

END OF UNIT - Review

Read. Write.

Dr. M. Jones
4536 S. North Ave.
San Diego
555-1967

Your next appointment is scheduled for:

Fri. Jan. 11 at 2:45

1. Date _____
2. Time _____
3. Doctor's name _____
4. Phone number _____

LUKE'S FINE FOOD STORE

558-8160

```
BAKERY          1.25
9/L KIT TUNA     .39
FNCY TN-SARD     .40
GRN VG/HAM       .34
GRB VG/BEEF      .34
GRB VG/TRKY      .34
HH WHIP CRM      .69
GRB VG/TRKY      .34
DAN PLAINYG     2.35

TAX   .17  BALANCE   6.61
CASH 20.01 CHANGE   13.40

12/22/89 10:18 AM 005   9    64
SEASONS GREETINGS!
```

1. Date _____
2. Time _____
3. Total _____
4. Change _____
5. Phone number _____
6. Name of store _____

EDISON ELECTRIC BILL
Box 14639
Chicago, IL 60657

```
423014A5
SERVICE  10-15 TO 11-13 DUE 12-06-89
FROM

RATE  PRESENT      KILOWATT
      READING      HOURS      AMOUNT
1     5089            641     48.62
          BULB SERVICE        .87
            STATE TAX        2.51
           AMOUNT DUE       52.00


THIS BILL IS FOR  29 DAYS
OF SERVICE FOR AN AVERAGE
DAILY COST OF $1.79
ACCOUNT NO. 4153407
```

1. Date due _____
2. Amount due _____
3. Bill _____

Read and write.

1.

```
205786 203762
ROAST BEEF
DELI

        | NET WT/CT | UNIT PRICE | TOTAL PRICE
DEC     |  0.65lb   |   5.78     |   $3.76
17
```

Date _____

Amount _____

Total price _____

Food _____

2.

```
KIDNEY BEANS

NET WEIGHT          PRICE/LB
 0.54 lbs            $1.09
                     $0.59

209970 800591
PACKED ON  DEC 20,89
```

Date _____

Amount _____

Total price _____

Food _____

3.

```
CHEESE

SHARP CHEDDAR
OVER 10 MONTHS OLD

SELL BY  | DELI | S/LB | NET
DEC.26.89|      | 3.39 | 0.67
                         0.02
                  TOTAL PRICE
                     2.27
0 208960 602276
```

Date _____

Amount _____

Total price _____

Food _____

4.

```
CHICKEN
                  SELL BY
                  12-19-89
NET WT./COUNT  UNIT PRICE  TOTAL PRICE
  2.41 lb       $0.99        $2.39
                           MEAT
200703 202392
SATISFACTION GUARANTEED
```

Date _____

Amount _____

Total price _____

Food _____

END OF UNIT - Find The Information.

Work with another student.

Circle the words you know.

LUCKY ELECTRONIC STORE
5637 First Street
York Town Shopping Mall
563-9100

SALE

Sat. Dec. 9 & Sun. Dec. 10 ONLY!

9 AM - 9 PM

13 inch Color Television
Compact portable with contrast picture tube. Model T-3461-76.

$199 *(Reg. $249)*

Electric Alarm Clock
White case with black numbers. Model 45-190

$4.99 *(Reg. $7.99)*

Stereo Cassette Recorder
Microphone, 4 speakers. Uses batteries or electricity.

$49.99 *(Reg. $55.99)*

Read. Write.

1. Name of the store: _____

2. Address of the store: _____

3. Phone Number: _____

4. Dates of the sale: _____

5. Days of the sale: _____

6. Time of the sale: _____

7. Sale price of a TV: _____

8. Sale price of a recorder: _____

9. Regular price of a recorder: _____

22: SCHOOL

Listen to the teacher.

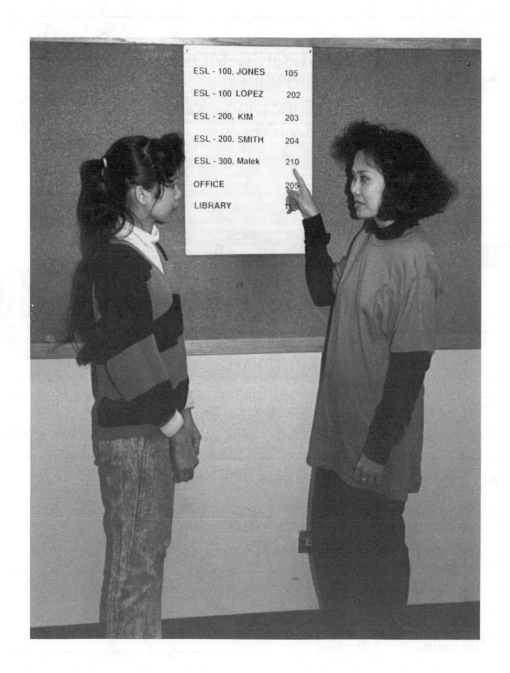

ESL - 100, JONES   105

ESL - 100 LOPEZ   202

ESL - 200, KIM   203

ESL - 200, SMITH   204

ESL - 300, Malek   210

OFFICE   205

LIBRARY

Practice with the teacher.

Read. Fill in. Copy.

school   __ __ __ __ __ __   _____

READING PRACTICE.

Say the words.

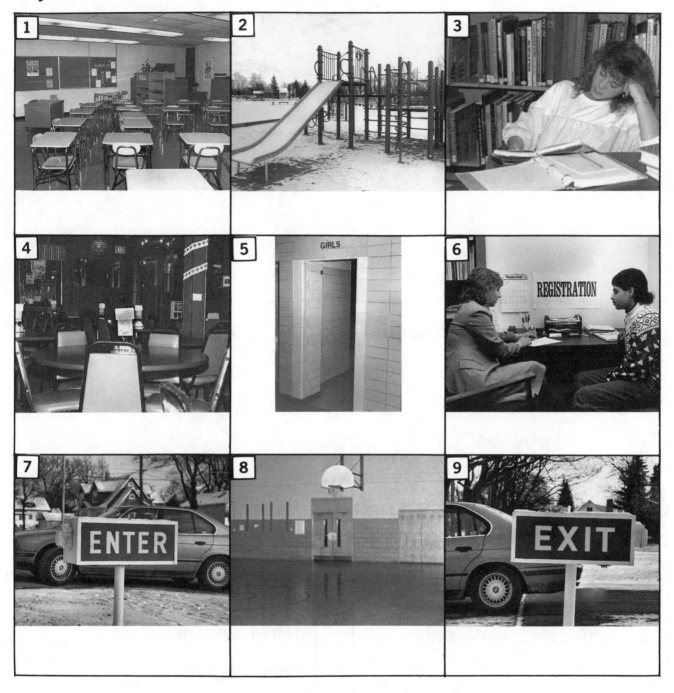

Read. Write the numbers next to the words.

_____ enter   _____ restrooms   _____ gym   _____ exit

_____ classroom   _____ playground   _____ library   _____ office

_____ cafeteria

Write the words under the pictures.

Say the words.

RESTROOMS

_____

_____

_____

_____

Read. Write the words under the pictures.

men   girls   women   boys

LETTER AND SOUND PRACTICE.

Write the words with M.

m __ __

__ __ m __ __

__ __ m

__ __ __ __ __ __ __ __ m

Write other words with M.

m __ __ __ __ __   name

father and m __ __ __ __ __

coffee with m __ __ __

Sun., M __ __., Tues.

Write the words with C.

c __ __ __ __ __ __ __ __

c __ __ __ __ __ __ __ __ __

Write other words with C.

zip c __ __ __

open or c __ __ __ __ __ __

103

READING PRACTICE.

Read.

SCHOOL DIRECTORY

Boys' Restroom	107
Cafeteria	102
Classrooms	105, 106, 109, 110, 111, 113, 114, 115
Girls' Restroom	108
Gym	103
Library	104
Office	100
Principal	101
Teachers' Room	112

Write the names of the rooms on the map.

103	104		112
102	105	109	113
101	106	110	114
100	107 · 108 · 111		115

Make a map of your school on a piece of paper.

SPEAKING PRACTICE.
Practice with a student.

Excuse me, where is <u>ESL 300</u>?   <u>Room 210.</u>

Thank you.   You're welcome.

Student A   **Student B**

Excuse me, where is the _____?   _____.

Thank you.   You're welcome.

1. Excuse me, ... library   Room 202.

2. Excuse me, ... gym   Room 100.

3. Excuse me, ... English class   Room 359.

4. Excuse me, ... office   Room 2.

5. Excuse me, ... cafeteria   Room 10.

6. Make your own conversation.   Make your own conversation.

23: POST OFFICE

Listen to the teacher.

Practice with the teacher.

Read. Fill in. Copy.

post office   __ o __ __   o __ __ i c e _____

READING PRACTICE.

Say the words.

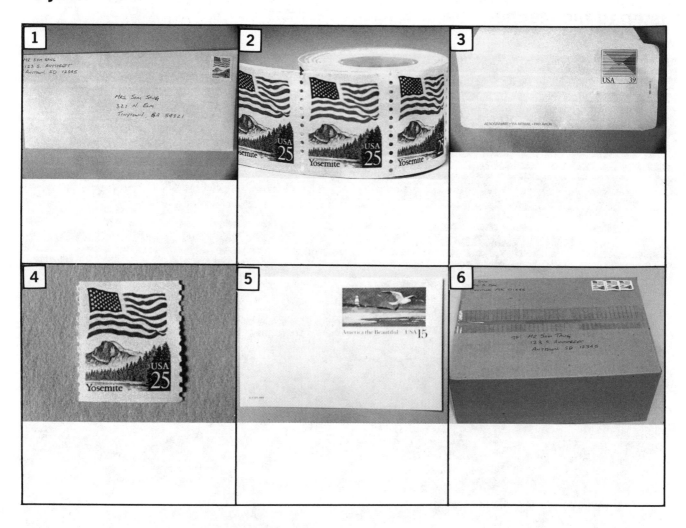

Read. Write the numbers next to the words.

_____ letter   _____ package   _____ stamp

_____ postcard   _____ aerogram   _____ roll of stamps

Read.

SPECIAL DELIVERY   OUT OF TOWN   FOREIGN AIR MAIL

LOCAL POSTMARK ONLY

SPEAKING PRACTICE.
Practice with a student.

Customer   Clerk

I'd like to <u>mail this letter</u>.   That's <u>$.65</u>. Is that all?

Yes. Here's <u>$1.00</u>.   Here's your change.

Thank you.   You're welcome. Have a nice day.

Student A   **Student B**

I'd like to _____.   That's _____. Is that all?

Yes. Here's _____.   Here's your change.

Thank you.   You're welcome.

1. I'd ... mail this package $10.25
   $15.00 $4.75

2. I'd ... mail this letter $.45
   $.50 $.05

3. I'd ... buy a roll of stamps $25.00
   $30.00 $5.00

4. I'd ... buy four post cards $.60
   $1.00 $.40

5. Make your own conversation.   Make your own conversation.

SPEAKING PRACTICE.

Listen to your teacher.

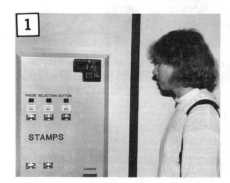

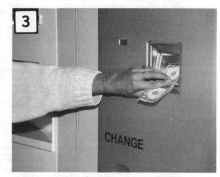

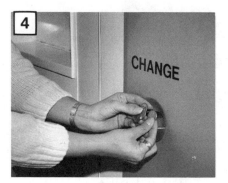

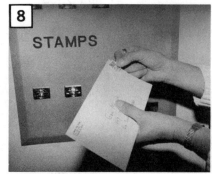

Say the instructions.

READING PRACTICE.

Read and do.

1. Go to the stamp machine.
2. Take out $1.00.
3. Put $1.00 in the change machine.
4. Take out your change.
5. Put one quarter in the stamp machine.
6. Press the button.
7. Take the 25¢ stamp.
8. Put the stamp on the letter.
9. Mail the letter.

Read and write.

1. Go to the stamp m __ __ __ __ __ __.
2. T __ __ __ out $ __ . __ __.
3. Put $1.00 in the change m __ __ __ __ __ __.
4. Take out your ch __ __ __ __.
5. Put one quarter in the stamp m __ __ __ __ __ __.
6. Press the __ __ t t __ __.
7. Take the 25¢ st __ __ __.
8. Put the st __ __ __ on the __ __ t t __ __.
9. M __ __ __ the letter.

Copy the sentences on a piece of paper.

24: BANK

Listen to the teacher.

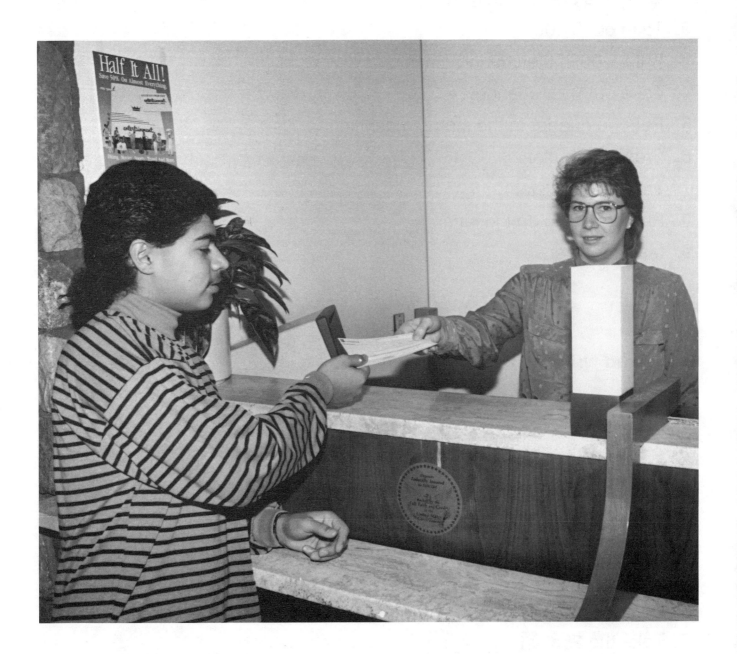

Practice with the teacher.

Read. Fill in. Copy.

bank   __ a n __   _____

READING PRACTICE.

Circle DEPOSIT.

Washington State Bank

DEPOSIT SAVINGS OR CHECKING

DATE	ACCOUNT NUMBER
Nov. 23, '90	203-413-81

LIST EACH CHECK SEPARATELY BY BANK NUMBER

TYPE	DOLLARS	CENTS
CASH	50	00
CHECKS	150	00
	75	70
TOTAL FROM OTHER SIDE		
SUBTOTAL	275	70
LESS CASH RECEIVED	—	
NET DEPOSIT	275	70

We have determined the expected number of days we must wait to receive final payment for various types of checks and instruments that are deposited by our customers. We may, therefore, place a "hold" on your account for the amount of a deposit. Our staff will notify you of the number of days a hold will be in place.

BE SURE EACH ITEM IS PROPERLY ENDORSED

USE OTHER SIDE FOR ADDITIONAL LISTING

S0085 (R08/1287)

1. Date _____

2. Amount _____

Fill out the deposit slip for fifty dollars ($50.00) cash.

Washington State Bank

DEPOSIT SAVINGS OR CHECKING

DATE	ACCOUNT NUMBER
	10346

LIST EACH CHECK SEPARATELY BY BANK NUMBER

TYPE	DOLLARS	CENTS
CASH		
CHECKS		
TOTAL FROM OTHER SIDE		
SUBTOTAL		
LESS CASH RECEIVED		
NET DEPOSIT		

We have determined the expected number of days we must wait to receive final payment for various types of checks and instruments that are deposited by our customers. We may, therefore, place a "hold" on your account for the amount of a deposit. Our staff will notify you of the number of days a hold will be in place.

BE SURE EACH ITEM IS PROPERLY ENDORSED

USE OTHER SIDE FOR ADDITIONAL LISTING

S0085 (R08/1287)

Circle WITHDRAWAL.

Washington State Bank

WITHDRAWAL SAVINGS OR CHECKING

DATE April 4, 1989   ACCOUNT NUMBER 325-30-82

[X] CASH   [ ] CHECK

MAKE CHECK PAYABLE TO

I HEREBY REQUEST A WITHDRAWAL FROM MY ACCOUNT AND ACKNOWLEDGE RECEIPT OF THIS SUM

One hundred   DOLLARS $ 100.00

TO BE SIGNED IN THE PRESENCE OF THE TELLER   SIGNATURE   Chun Lee

S0116 (R04/0786)

1. Amount _____

2. Date _____

Fill out the withdrawal slip for twenty-five dollars ($25.00) cash.

Washington State Bank

WITHDRAWAL SAVINGS OR CHECKING

DATE   ACCOUNT NUMBER 23-106

[ ] CASH   [ ] CHECK

MAKE CHECK PAYABLE TO

I HEREBY REQUEST A WITHDRAWAL FROM MY ACCOUNT AND ACKNOWLEDGE RECEIPT OF THIS SUM

DOLLARS $

TO BE SIGNED IN THE PRESENCE OF THE TELLER   SIGNATURE

S0116 (R04/0786)

SPEAKING PRACTICE.
Practice with a student.

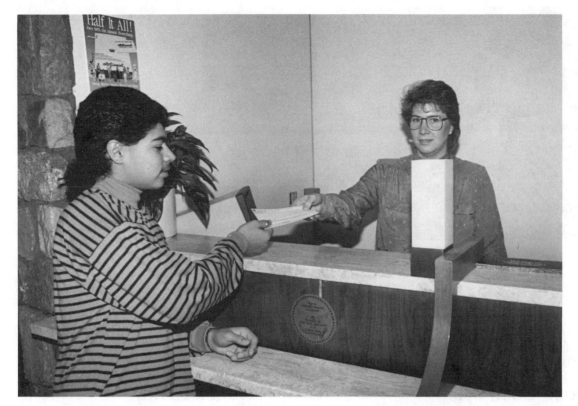

Customer   Bank Teller

I'd like to <u>deposit $40.00.</u>   Thank you. Here's your receipt.
Thank you.   Have a nice day.

Student A   **Student B**

I'd like to _____.   Thank you. Here's your receipt.
Thank you.   You're welcome.

1. I'd ... deposit $75.00

2. I'd ... deposit $200.00

3. I'd ... deposit $100.00

4. I'd ... deposit $250.00

5. I'd ... deposit my paycheck

6. Make your own conversation.   Make your own conversation.

SPEAKING PRACTICE.
Practice with a student.

Customer   Bank Teller

Customer	Bank Teller
I'd like to <u>withdraw $25.00.</u>	Do you have any identification?
Here's my <u>driver's license.</u>	Thank you. Here's <u>$25.00.</u>
Thank you. Good-bye.	Have a nice day.

Student A   **Student B**

Student A	Student B
I'd like to _____.	Do you have any identification?
Here's my _____.	Thank you. Here's _____.
Thank you. Good-bye.	Have a nice day.

1. I'd ... withdraw $50.00
   driver's license $50.00

2. I'd ... withdraw $90.00
   driver's license and a credit card $90.00

3. I'd ... withdraw $700.00
   I-94 card $700.00

4. I'd ... withdraw $1000.00
   driver's license and a passport $1000.00

5. Make your own conversation.   Make your own conversation.

25: TRANSPORTATION

Listen to the teacher.

Practice with the teacher.

Read. Fill in. Copy.

bus   __ u __   _____

READ. FILL IN. COPY.

STOP   __ __ O P

_____

BUS STOP   __ U S   S T O __

_____

WALK   __ A L K

_____

DON'T WALK   __ O N'T W A L __

_____

Other transportation words: TRAIN   TAXI   SUBWAY

117

LETTER AND SOUND PRACTICE.

Write the words with ST.   **Write other words with ST.**

s t __ __

__ __ __   s t __ __

city and st __ __ __

Air Mail st __ __ __

Write a word with W.   **Write another word with W.**

w __ __ __

man and w __ __ __ __

Write the words with T.   **Write other words with T.**

t __ __ __

t __ __ __ __

chair and t __ __ __ __

students and t __ __ __ __ __ __

t __ __ __ __ __ __ __ __ number

READING PRACTICE.

Read. Write the words under the pictures.

STOP   WALK   DON'T WALK

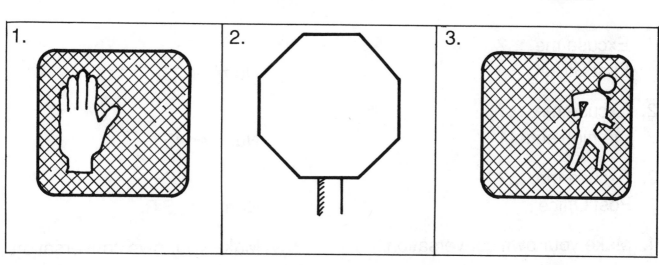

1.

2.

3.

SPEAKING PRACTICE.

Practice with a student.

Excuse me, can you help me?   Yes.

I want to go to _the library._

Which bus do I take?   _Number 693._

Thank you.   You're welcome.

Student A   **Student B**

Excuse me, can you help me?   Yes.

I want to go to _____.

Which bus do I take?   _____.

Thank you.   You're welcome.

1. Excuse me, ...?
    First Street   Number 25.

2. Excuse me, ...?
    the high school   Number 45.

3. Excuse me, ...?
    Post Office   Number 15 B.

4. Make your own conversation.   Make your own conversation.

END OF UNIT - Review

Read and write.

PHONE   STOP   WALK   MEN   DON'T WALK

WOMEN   BOYS   GIRLS   TELEPHONE

1.	2.
_____	_____
3.	4.
_____	_____
5.	6.
_____	_____

120

END OF UNIT - New Situation

Write a money order to the Phone Company.

Money Order
2931 349

DATE _12/26/89_ 75-53/919

PAY TO THE ORDER OF _____

=NOT VALID FOR OVER THREE HUNDRED U.S. DOLLARS=

25 DOLS 00 CTS

AMOUNT   DOLLARS

SIGNATURE   ADDRESS
BY SIGNING YOU AGREE TO THE SERVICE CHARGE AND OTHER TERMS ON THE REVERSE SIDE.

005331:303 29313498⑴ 90

Write a money order to the Gas Company.

DO NOT PAY OVER FIFTY DOLLARS

Money Order
903 2303 34

DATE _2/ 6/89_ 75-53/919

PAY TO THE ORDER OF _____

=NOT VALID FOR OVER THREE HUNDRED U.S. DOLLARS=

5 DOLS 00 CTS

AMOUNT   DOLLARS

SIGNATURE   ADDRESS
BY SIGNING YOU AGREE TO THE SERVICE CHARGE AND OTHER TERMS ON THE REVERSE SIDE.

⑴091900533⑴303

Write a check for ten dollars to your school.

151

_____19_____ 70-886/719

PAY TO THE ORDER OF_____ $ _____

_____ DOLLARS

SUBURBAN BANK

MEMO_____ _____

⑴0719088 15⑴ 01

END OF UNIT - New Situation

Circle the amount due. Write a check for fifteen dollars.

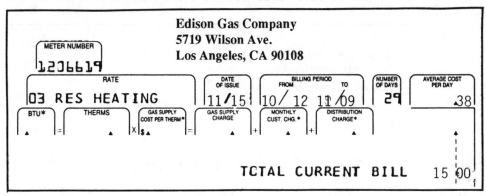

Edison Gas Company
5719 Wilson Ave.
Los Angeles, CA 90108

METER NUMBER
1236619

RATE	DATE OF ISSUE	BILLING PERIOD FROM	TO	NUMBER OF DAYS	AVERAGE COST PER DAY
03 RES HEATING	11/15	10/12	11/09	29	.38

BTU*		THERMS		GAS SUPPLY COST PER THERM*	GAS SUPPLY CHARGE		MONTHLY CUST. CHG. *		DISTRIBUTION CHARGE*
▲	=	▲	X $▲	=	▲	+	▲	+	▲

TOTAL CURRENT BILL   15 00

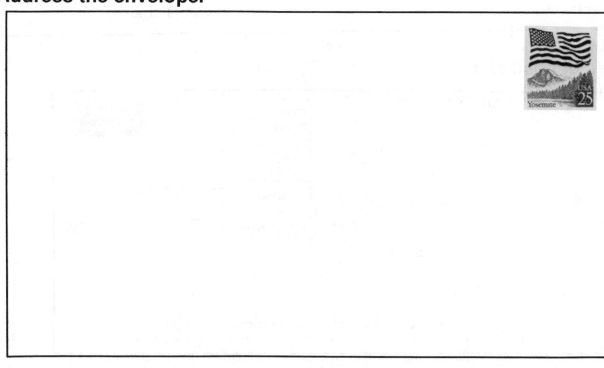

776

——————————— 19 ———   70-72932719

PAY TO THE ORDER OF _____ $ [   ]

_____ DOLLARS

FIRST BANK
A FEDERAL SAVINGS BANK

FOR _____

972938 018100

Address the envelope.

END OF UNIT - Find The Information.

Work with another student.

Circle the words you know.

Lincoln Furniture Factory
1645 Western Ave.
Brook Heights, MN 55104

No. 4625

Manuel Ramirez
SS #: 353-00-0001

Date 05/31/89	Description	Current Check	Year To Date
	Gross Pay	509.59	5095.00
	Federal Tax	59.00	590.00
	F.I.C.A.	38.22	382.22
	State Tax	35.67	356.70
	Take Home Pay	376.70	3767.00

Lincoln Furniture Factory
1645 Western Ave.
Brook Heights, MN 55104

No. 4625

May 31, 1990

Pay to the
Order of

Manuel Ramirez $509.59

FIVE HUNDRED NINE DOLLARS AND FIFTY NINE CENTS

SECOND NATIONAL BANK

1:69684:4536:0

M. T. Kohn
Authorized Signature

Write a deposit slip.

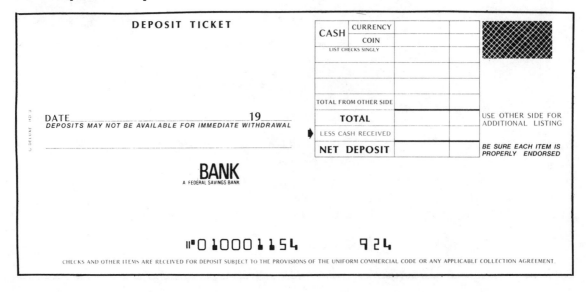

END OF UNIT - Find The Information.

Work with another student.

Circle the words you know.

CITY BUS FARES

Adult -	$.75
Child (2 yrs. - 12 yrs.) -	$.25
Child (under 2 yrs.) -	Free

Transfers Transfers *Must be purchased with the ticket!*

Adult -	$.25
Child -	Free

Fares must be exact. NO CHANGE is given on the bus.

Monthly Pass

Adult -	$30.00
Child (2 yrs. - 12 yrs.) -	$15.00

1ST BANK
300 Main Street
El Paso

ACCOUNT NUMBER

1006385

DEPOSIT RECEIPT

OCT14-89 NDP   9:57   812.14

THE AMOUNT ON THIS RECEIPT WILL BE POSTED IN YOUR PASSBOOK
OR WILL APPEAR ON YOUR NEXT STATEMENT.

FIRST WORDS provides nonliterate and semi-literate secondary and adult students with basic survival oral and literacy skills so that they can minimally manage their life skill needs in both school and community settings.

CONTENTS

FIRST WORDS consists of three books: the Student Book, the Teacher Book, and the Teacher Resource Book and a cassette tape.

The **Teacher Book** is designed for the teacher who would like specific instructions for teaching each activity. In addition to the step-by-step instructions, it contains an introduction to the book and the script for the listening activities.

The **Teacher Resource Book** contains the introduction to the book, the script for the listening activities, and a variety of reproducible worksheets which provide extra practice for the less able student and more challenging practice for the more able student.

The **tape** contains the listening activities and the dialogs.

FIRST WORDS contains 25 lessons. Seven of these focus on the "building blocks" of print literacy --- alphabet, numbers, money, time, and dates. The remaining lessons spiral in these building blocks and integrate them with oral language competencies. These lessons consist of three phases: Oral Practice, Printed Practice, and Oral and Printed Practice. The steps are listed below:

ORAL PRACTICE

- Preproduction
- Early Production
- Lesson Introduction
- Dialog
- Interaction

PRINTED PRACTICE

- Introduction to print
- Practice

ORAL and PRINTED PRACTICE

- Re-introduction of the dialog in printed form
- Practice in reading the dialog
- Pair practice

METHODOLOGY

The first phase of the lesson is the most critical part of the lesson because it establishes the context and introduces the target language in a comprehensible manner. In the Student Book, this phase is called "Listen To Your Teacher/Practice With Your Teacher" and it relies upon the initial large photo. *NOTE: The script for these activities is found in both the Teacher Book and the Teacher Resource Book.*

Oral Practice:

Preproduction: The teacher provides comprehensible input by describing the photo. Then, the teacher checks students' comprehension by asking them to point to various objects or activities in the photo. For example, on page 1, the script begins with the teacher saying,

> *"There are two people. They are at school. They are in an office. They are in an office at school. etc."*
> *"Point to the student. Point to the woman. etc."*

Early Production: The teacher asks Yes/No questions about the photo. Then, the teacher progresses to asking "or" questions and concludes with simple "Wh" questions with students responding in short phrases. To continue the above example, the teacher would ask,

> *"Are they at school? Are they in the office? etc."*
> *"Are they in the office or in the classroom? etc."*
> *"Where are the teacher and the student? etc."*

Lesson Introduction: The teacher introduces the topic.

Dialog: The teacher models the dialog, with students later practicing the dialog orally.

Interaction: The teacher guides students in personalizing and extending the dialog.

Printed Practice:

The teacher explains and guides students through each activity. (See the Teacher Book for instructions.)

Oral and Printed Practice:

The teacher explains and guides students through each activity. (See the Teacher Book for specific instructions.)

FIRST WORDS, Linda Mrowicki
Linmore Publishing, Box 1545, Palatine, IL 60078
(800) 336-3656

Student Book	ISBN 0-916591-21-2
Teacher Book	ISBN 0-916591-25-5
Teacher Resource Book	ISBN 0-916591-22-0
Cassette Tape	ISBN 0-916591-31-X